The Sons of Chester

A Tale of Small Town Boys, Baseball, and Very Big Dreams

Craig Ohlau & Kevin L. Gingrich

Black Rose Writing | Texas

ISBN: 978-1-68433-214-4
PUBLISHED BY BLACK ROSE WRITING
www.blackrosewriting.com

Printed in the United States of America
Suggested Retail Price (SRP) $19.95

The Sons of Chester is printed in Palatino Linotype

For Danny. And Peyton. Father. Son.

This is the story of dreaming and whether dreams come true. In the summer of 1995, my "brothers" and I chased after our dream of a national championship. And after that, we kept dreaming. This is the story of the dreams and the town that made them possible.

—Craig "Bobber" Ohlau

Praise for
The Sons of Chester

"For every kid who ever picked up a bat and dreamed of hitting a home run, *este libro te tocará las venas de tu corazón.*"
— Bengie Molina, World Series Champion and author of New York Times Bestseller *Molina*

"This book is a real winner!"
— Gary Kaschak, author of *My Name was Mickey Mantle*

"In *The Sons of Chester*, Ohlau and Gingrich tap into the poetry of small-town America with their memoir of a high school baseball team's quest for a state championship. Layering the narrative with stories of the community—fathers and mothers, criminals and celebrities—the authors transform a fine sports story into a touching work of art."
— Brian Kaufman, author of *The Fat Lady's Low, Sad Song*

"Cardinal fans everywhere–from the big cities to the rural midwestern plains–will root all the way through for *The Sons of Chester.*"
— Jim Cromer, Host of *Two Birds on a Bat* Podcast

"Ohlau and Gingrich bring an unparalleled style in this memorable story of family, friends, and a town. They are as steady as the Mississippi flows."
— Tim Funkhouser, IHSA Coaching Hall of Famer

"*The Sons of Chester* is soft, amusing, and bittersweet, with a great narrative and inspirational storytelling. Ohlau and Gingrich have hit a moonshot out of the park!"
— Vernell Moehrs, Midwest Baseball Legend and National Semi-Pro Baseball Hall of Famer

"*The Sons of Chester* is a charitable nod to all that is forgivable. It is aimed at the chest of every kid who ever dreamed of being a champion and every father who dreamed of raising one and every coach who ever sought to lead a group of boys."

–Randy Wells, Chicago Cubs 2008-2012

"Ohlau and Gingrich find the heart in the heart of small-town America in this compellingly written tale. *The Sons of Chester* is more than merely the story of a group of boys clowning around and playing baseball in the 90s. It's the story of the town that made them, a town where their fathers and coaches work among the most notorious criminals in US history; a town of great characters, whose great-grandfathers and mothers inspired one of the most famous casts of characters of the 20th century."

–Brian "Gritty" Snider, *KSGM Radio*

"No baseball guy who reads *The Sons of Chester* will soon forget this wonderful tale. It is a time capsule into the last great decade of small-town American history."

–Matt Kamp, *Edwardsville Intelligencer*

"If you loved *Hoosiers*, *The Rookie,* or *A League of Their Own*, then you'll love this true story. Beautifully written and told, *The Sons of Chester* captures the essence of small-town, baseball-loving boys and their quest to win it all. Profoundly entertaining, *The Sons of Chester* reminds us of what it takes to win, and equally, of what it takes to lose. You'll stand up and cheer."

–Gary Kaschak, author of *My Name was Mickey Mantle*

"I spent just nine years covering high school sports in the area, but I have no doubt Ohlau and Gingrich's book captures perfectly the experience of playing sports and daring to dream big while growing up in a small town in southern Illinois in the 1990s. The antics with friends, the battles with brothers, the love for baseball, even dad talking from the other side of the newspaper, are all memories that transcend the backdrop of Chester, one of Illinois' unique places. You don't have to be from Chester to enjoy this book."

–Jim Gordillo, High School Sportswriter
Bloomington Herald-Times

The Sons of Chester

PART ONE:
WELCOME TO CHESTER

PROLOGUE:
A POSSIBLE FENCE

In my hometown of Chester, Illinois, on the banks of the Mississippi, live 2,000 murderers. A thousand of them are legally insane. Growing up, my friends and I didn't care much about all that. Our minds were on one thing. Baseball. And girls. Well, two things.

—Craig "Bobber" Ohlau

Light and Swanwick

If you get on your bike at Light and Swanwick where the rough red brick, two-story home stands sturdy on the corner and head two porches down past St. Mary's church and school, red brick too, every gothic line and gutter painted white, and turn right onto Church Street, pedaling past your old stomping grounds, "St. Mary's Bowl" behind the church—a half-acre crater in the earth, as perfect as a colander, with slick grass hills you could almost sled down in the summer to a sandlot where five generations of Catholic schoolyard children have played, argued, and tamped the playground dirt, barefoot, Keds, Converse, and Nike, to crucible powder so that the bottom of the bowl looks like the thumbprint of God — and ride your bike past every little house and shameless trailer — new built homes in town still put on an open front porch and about everyone seems allowed exactly one sufficient shade tree and a yard just big enough the neighbor boy can push mow it for five bucks, or you may not be particular about the grass, like the Luthy's, where Mr. Luthy might be seen out rhythmically hitting grounders to his little boy who wears a baseball cap his head is still filling in — Chester itself laid out like a delta, twenty blocks wide at its best, sprawled out from the river bank beyond the bluff, not so much blocks, really, as contiguities of homes, on a warm summer night, the humidity from the river valley lingering over the bluff, you can ride a bike from house to house across town and never miss a pitch, the St. Louis Cardinal's broadcast issuing from every porch and living room, one generation to the next, the wafted communion of Cardinal's baseball like a ghost in the air — the "Ho-ly Cow!" of Harry Carey, the arrogant insouciance of Jack Buck, the beer sloshy side mouth of Mike Shannon — issuing from practically every house — you could ride your bike from Spring Street to Knapp and hear the whole bottom of the ninth — then turn left on Valley St., a long hill road, more country than town, crowded on both sides by elm trees lush and leaning over the road with confetti leaves cheering you on, and coast all the way down Bridge Bypass, the loose gravel of the little delta crunching beneath your tires, and lean in and circle down to the road that runs beneath it, to Kaskaskia St. — and you run into the river.

The Mississippi. Every time you see it, no matter where you cross over it, it takes you back to the town you grew up in, if you are from Chester, just like every fishing hole you fish in takes you back to the fishing holes of your youth, and every piece of cornbread from an iron skillet takes you back to your mom's kitchen, and every baseball field you see to the field you once played on as a kid. The Mississippi here is almost unremarkable to an outsider but not disappointing. Mistakably deep, army fatigue green waters move inconspicuously by, as much a part of the town and your mentality as an unconscious motive. In times of change, and times are always changing, the river runs unchanged. The same sight that took the young Samuel Clemens away, first in his spirit and imagination and then on a riverboat and then in his books, still flows by. It takes you away. And brings you home again—for Chester, for many reasons, is a hard town to leave.

Still to this day in sentimental homage a replica steamboat nuzzles up to the sandbar dock and lets tourists aboard—as if they were going somewhere to see something when townfolks wonder why anyone would get on a boat to see what has always been there and always will be, but apparently things that don't change are a source of wonder to tourists.

The steel, {-shaped bridge to Perry County spanning the river to Missouri looks like it was built by an engineer who never outgrew erector sets. A man's work is his play; a boy's play is his work. Its shadow lays a stripe across the river and barges skim along the water as surreptitiously as crocodiles on the Nile, pulling great freights of disemboweled raw materials. But the little side thought of Chester has some ambition as more than a place to pass by and pass through. At least it does to you. You're headed somewhere.

Barges skim along the water like crocodiles on the Nile

Down Kaskaskia Street you go, a street so innocently named you'd think you'd see Beezus and Ramona playing jacks on the sidewalk. In truth, the street is named for the ancient state capital, for more than a century the cultural and commercial capital of Illinois, once the metropolis of the Mississippi Valley, nine miles upstream, and now a cursed island, population 14, *fourteen*, for the river once impetuously shifted and cut off the little ill-planned peninsula town.

The lonely river and the lonely road and the lonely railroad tracks between run side by side until soon the stately, sad brown, time-forsaken brick comes into view. You sense you are approaching the past. The river runs past you. Ahead, a twelve-foot fence as natural as a baseball backstop but for the silver, perfectly spiraled razor wire gives a slightly confining impression. You ride directly past the large parking lots in front of the prison. Two somber and oddly inattentive lions, sphinx-like and suffering erosion and made of the same material as the prison house, flank the wide driveway. Welcome to the Menard State Penitentiary.

The Menard maximum security prison, built during the Civil War and renamed honorifically for John Willis Menard, the first African American to be elected to the United States Congress, was given the eerily optimistic name "Menard Correctional Center," connotations as benign as a rec facility. Except for the roaming in the prison yard of prisoners, some of America's most incorrigible criminals, there's not much re-creation at Menard.

Some townsfolk, when asked about Illinois' largest maximum security prison, the state's second oldest, speak proudly. They tell you how the prison was featured in two rather famous movies, the 1967 Academy Award-winning *In the Heat of the Night*, with the at-odds greats Rod Steiger and Sidney Poitier—and a very steamy window peeping scene; and the 1993 movie *The Fugitive*, starring Harrison Ford. Chester, with its own contradictions of ominous and innocence—prison and cake mix factory, beer taverns and dairy—proved better than Hollywood set designers had imagined.

You stand up on your bike and glance over at the few inmates in the yard out for their hour of recreation in orange jumpsuits. Some of them are big from weightlifting and seem practically harmless for the hardening. Through a fortress of fences intelligently constructed to inspire not the least thought of escape, you see inside the pen. Your dad is in there. He works the prison. He works at Menard. He guards the most dangerous men in America.

You've seen him come home with blood on his shirt. He won't talk about it.

In Chester, Illinois, on the banks of the Mississippi River, live 2,000 murderers, a thousand of them legally insane. It's the best concentration of killers of any place in the United States and almost a quarter the population of Chester itself. Watching over them, guarding them, monitoring their every activity, and preventing their escape, are 134 guards, mostly local men, fathers and brothers, from the little town of

Chester, the good residents of Chester, Illinois. Altercations are part of the job.

You remember the day of one incident vaguely. Somehow, on the cold February morning in the exact middle of the month, 1983, the notorious I-57 killer Henry Brisbon, Jr., on death row at Menard, managed to slip out of handcuffs, break away from a guard, take a makeshift knife and attempt to, as he had earlier sworn, kill fellow convicted serial killer John Wayne Gacy. Gacy, the most notorious criminal in Illinois history after Al Capone, had been convicted of multiple murders, the bodies of 33 of his victims found buried in the crawl space of his suburban Chicago home. Many of them were boys, strangled.

You stand up on your bike, the glove on the handlebars knocking your knee. You have places to go.

So Brisbon lunged. One of the dads grabbed him. Gacy was barely hurt in the attack. Nobody there working the prison that day much remembers the incident. Your dad barely spoke of it, but you heard him mutter something to Mom.

Gacy was eventually transported to another facility, where they gave him and his family a picnic lunch. It was his last meal. They executed him that night.

The prison stands on the floodplain, a good stone's throw—or rather, a long home run—away from the Mississippi, so near the river that the Great Flood of 1993 inundated everything but the top of the watchtower, which stood out above the waters like Noah's ark. In the courtyard, you're on a level with the river but without all the advantages of the view. Nothing discourages a view like a prison fence. It's the razor wire. Spirals of it, as purposefully festooned as an Independence Day decoration, shred the sunlight.

The Great Flood of 1993 inundated everything but the top of the watchtower, which stood out above the waters like Noah's ark.

Inmates in orange jumpsuits mill about in the yard. Some walk like dead men. One killed his mother. Another butchered a man he didn't even have an argument with. They are banished from all society but their own. Their closest friends are rapists and serial murderers. They are surrounded by walls and fences with machine gun-bearing guards watching, a brutally restrictive perimeter. They live under threats so institutionalized they have bounded their very imaginations. Walls and fences that there is no other side to hold them as much subconsciously as physically. There is nothing beyond the fences but the timeless Mississippi streaming by in sameness. Nothing qualifies a view like a good fence. Theirs is an impossible fence.

Fences and walls thick and impossible separate the men from their dreams. Inside they lie on naked bunks. At night behind impregnable walls they lie in claustrophobic cells on bare bunks like dead men. They have dreams. They just cannot follow them.

But you are following yours. You have somewhere to get to. You rise up on your bike. You stand up on the pedals and churn side to side, your knees knocking against the leather on your handlebars. To your left, the mighty Mississippi flows on its own way, a deceptive light sheen of green gliding along like a treadmill. You know of boys who have drowned in that deception. But you cannot entirely fear things that bring life to the town, and that cannot be changed. You ride past red brick warehouses with hundreds of cracked-glazing transom windows cracked open uncomfortably close to the road — an inmate might reach out and grab a boy off a bike... Naw, they're just warehouses for storage.

A half mile more on Kaskaskia St., little more than a bike trail at this point, and you turn back up the bluff, onto Fern Valley Road, an uphill, scenic, well-manicured roadside (kept by prisoners themselves kept under guard), a paved path cutting narrowly through the state-owned woods. The property leads to the top of the bluff and the good and spacious land of Illinois. You lift off your bike, churn right to left, lean over your bike Lance-Armstrong like, your legs burning, to the open field and flatness of Route 3, the fastest way out of town. Your parents don't want you riding far on the highway;

that's why you took the safer route, the detour past the prison where your dad works.

The Menard Correctional Center is far behind you now and down the bluff. But it's perhaps not the worst place in Chester. Over there, back behind the woods is the worst place, a distinction that belongs to the Mental Health Center, the only facility in Illinois capable of housing criminals found "unfit to stand trial" or "not guilty by reason of insanity."

You remember the most frightening sleepover joke of all time: An inmate from the asylum has escaped — he's a murderer and mentally insane. That night, for comfort you reach down and pet your dog on the floor by your bed, who gives your hand the reassuring lick. The next morning you find your dog and your whole family *butchered* and a note that reads, "Crazies can lick too." That punchline will make you shudder thirty years later.

Menard Correctional Center and the Mental Health Center are the two main employers in town. They are where the majority of townspeople from Chester work. Prudently, neither place is mentioned on the Chester website.

You ride on. You have somewhere to get to. The sun is shining, and the wind is whipping the first scents of springtime off the bluff. And springtime means one thing to you...

You ride on the shoulder of Route 3, on the left side so semis don't sneak up behind and abduct you in their wake. Route 3 is the main artery of all of southwestern

Illinois. It scribbles along from Cairo in the south to just north of the nexus of metro-east St. Louis, parallel to that ruder and more romantic route, the Mississippi herself. The Great River Road as it is known zigzags right through the heart of Chester, one block from Light and Swanwick. At night, you hear the fleets of semis go by as little Sam Clemens once heard riverboats.

Your legs are no longer burning. You're on flat high ground. The excitement is building. You have left the prison far behind; ahead is another facility bounded by fence. This one you come to with heart pounding. This one you enter at your will and leave against it. This one is a place of dreams. This is where the dream of a baseball flying over the left field fence comes true, where the crowd, come as to a family reunion, sits happily in lawn chairs, Grampas and Grammas as content as were the summer crop already harvested, more fulfilled than were they at a graduation party. There goes up the intermittent, small but very personal eruption of cheering in the summer air. The smell of hotdogs and hot oiled popcorn. The smell of dirt and leather and wood and sweat. Every basic element that made America, including courage. It's some people's favorite outing. It used to be America's favorite game. It still is yours. Baseball.

The younger children playing in the grass outside the field are pretending to be you. Your name is Craig, but everybody calls you "Bobber." You bat third, and you're a starting pitcher. You have a dream. The big leagues. The World Series.

You're twelve years old.

The stretches and clutter of woods along Rt. 3 yield to one large multi-acre opening, with low fences. These are the ball fields of Gordon "Bud" Cohen Recreational Complex, named for a local sports enthusiast who left a lot of money to build a field of dreams at a time when corn and soybean prices gave little hope to small farmers. The complex is as purposefully cut from the woods as the work of a German immigrant in the late nineteenth century with one lumber saw and ax clearing timber made a field for corn. This is a different kind of field. A field far from the prison. A field surrounded by fence. A field of dreams. Here the infields were plucked of every tree and stump and picked of every field stone and pebble and grated as smooth as a tabletop by a little tractor that will never see a farm dragging a section of chain link fence. The outfields are the best-kept lawns in the county, clean as the living room floor on which you practiced the Mickey Mantle hook slide your dad taught you.

They will add, in the years to come, softball fields for girls and soccer fields that will forever feel *European*, and a walking track with different checkpoints for exercise for the elderly and for those for whom exercise is no longer the necessity of play, and a running path that orbits it all. But it's the perfect geometries of the *baseball fields* that are the center of your universe.

Cohen is what you get when sandlots are turned into visions: perfectly kept grounds and the distinctive mark of every baseball stadium, a boundless perimeter, a goal, a dream—a fence. This fence you can get over. This fence is not a restriction but a goal, not a confinement but a calling. This is a possible fence.

Some day you will hit a home run over it that will spill popcorn and make everyone clap and make a sound that sounds like the start of a scream and bring Grampa sitting up in his lawn chair and make your mother bounce on her toes and your dad nod in the well-satisfied certainty that he has taught you right. And you will round the bases, glancing after the ball lost on the far side of the fence that children chase like a rumored Easter egg. Everyone looks briefly over the fence. Nothing encourages a view like a good fence. Fly balls fly over fences like dreams.

You get off your bike. It's baseball practice.

You slide the leather glove off the handlebars which has been like a ballast the whole ride. Some mothers drop their kids off in vans and old cars. The coaches pull up in pickup trucks. They are overweight men with potbellies who breathe through their noses and make their nose hairs twitter, who somewhere earned the right to show you how the game is to be done. They have the bats and balls for practice. It's hard to imagine sometimes how some of these men, now misshaped, regular drinkers, ever rounded the bases to stretch out a double. But some of them are legends in town for what they did on a baseball field under the sole scrutiny of the sun or the white lights of a night game.

Cohen Field is not where the dream started. That would have been back in town down in St. Mary's Bowl, a pickup game with girls included and then excluded as you got older and meaner and more determined about your dream. The dream started while daydreaming during Social Studies. On a summer night sleepover just goofing around was when the idea came. It just slipped out, just popped out as loosely as a joke, an inchoate dream—that suddenly stopped everyone with its severity and truth, the wonder of it, the possibility. The next morning it was still there. It did not dissipate with the morning fog off the river. It grew more clear in the hot sun. The dream dogs your days. The dream carries you through long hours of school in confining desks that you feel like you want to stretch the axle off and pull apart or turn into some kind of racecar. The dream is to win a national championship.

It has never been done before, not in your world. In the whole history of the town, in the whole history of southern Illinois, no one ever won a *national* championship. No one was ever presumptuous enough to chase that dream. Small towns are not usually made of dreamers. There are more machiners in Chester than dreamers.

You pound your glove a couple of times to re-form it to your hand and walk toward the field. This is not where the dream started, not in Cohen Recreational Facility. But it is where it will be achieved. Baseball season is started.

You swing open the little gate in the fence that surrounds the field and the metal door whose metal catch is like a tuning fork chink against the pole. You are fenced in.

Your teammates are dropped off one by one or glide onto the beachhead of grass on their bikes and join you inside. The coaches have dumped out the bats from a large canvas bag that has carried like weapons bats since World War II. The wood of the bats and the aluminum of the bats tumbling out and hitting each other makes a sound you like. You know the aluminum bats like a hobbyist knows his models. There's the orange and black 31", 25 oz. Big Barrel C-Core Model; the 30", 24 oz. Scandium Easton Redline; the 36", 34 oz. Easton Black Magic Model 1990 that you will not be worthy of 'til you get your driver's license. The C-core and the Redline are considered sacred.

Even reckless boys have something they learn to touch gently. You pick out your bats with manners, more carefully than a No. 2 pencil, as if they were weapons of survival. You field ground balls like soldiers fighting for a town. *Crack crack crack,* one after the other the coaches test your defense. You learn to wait. You learn to stand like a man in the field. You learn to spit like a man. The squinting intensity of the game, the salt sweat and dust in your eyes—boys who cannot pay attention to Mrs. Langford's introduction to Trigonometry hold calm but searing attention on a 3–2 pitch. There's always an unpredictably and thus a regular immediacy in baseball. It's a game of hypnotic spells of inactivity—a horsefly in the outfield is almost a welcome distraction—then sudden emergency and momentary drama and the most parsimonious cheers.

Nothing is wasted. A fat kid's running out a grounder is considered no exercise in futility. A duel of wits turns into an explosive advantage, a catcall to an outrage, a tension to sudden relief, a split-second effort to fulfillment. You never know exactly when it will come. The pitcher conceals his intentions. The catcher glances furtively around. Spies are on the base path. The third base coach swipes two fingers across his chest in a gesture as religious as Saturday evening mass at St. Mary's. Sacrifice bunt. The batter effects a relaxed stance whose deception is the best lie he ever told. Baseball is a game of raw simplicity and gamesmanship. The baldest little battlefield, with one mound, one little patch of home to protect, one justly paranoid runner venturing among nine enemy players. And a fence. Eight hang their destinies, their entire summer of boyhood, on the arm of one man. He's twelve years old.

The instinct to throw comes natural to a boy. A toddler sees a rock, and he throws it. He picks up a rubber ball. His dad claps and coaxes him, "Throw it to, Daddy." It's the first confidence he feels by means of separation from his dad. He sees a river, and he thinks he can throw a stone across it. There's the story of the boy George Washington throwing a silver dollar across the Potomac. It doesn't matter whether it's legend or not. You know he thought he could do it.

He kicks a little trench on the mound, like a horse pawing at the dirt, as much out of imitation of the great men he has watched on TV as the need for some good footing today. He will be a mechanic, or a guard at the prison one day like his father, or he will buy the Chester Dairy, or will teach Math or Biology at the local high school, maybe fight wars like his grandpas. But today he is working — on the mound. He is not the hardest thrower. He is technical and savvy. He concentrates. He is the center of attention in a way that he will never be again his entire life, except on his wedding day. He reaches back to put his strength and artistry on the ball...

The pitch comes in, hissing high and tailing away. You know of fastballs so hard and heavy that if they ever nip your elbow, you'll fear the pain for the rest of the summer. Let a third strike by or throw errant down to second and you'll feel the pain for the rest of your life.

You hear the pitch as briefly as a bug. You have one fraction of a moment to make a decision and a dream come true.

The fields of Cohen are surrounded by fence not so terribly reminiscent of those of Menard down the bluff. For one thing, no razor wire. These fences hold promise. They look a mile away when you are twelve but possible when you're fourteen. With just the right pitch. Fat, as they say. Extend the bat and swing through with smooth acceleration of the bat. It's the smoothness of the swing, not the speed. Grace is power at perfect acceleration. God made the human eye to see the swinging of a bat at perfect acceleration as the most graceful of things a man can do without a woman. The bat catches the ball and lifts it skyward. There's an optimal angle, a trajectory that is so fulfilling you can't believe it came from your bat that is so much of an extension of you it warrants full pride. They are fences, you know full well, put up not to hold you in but to tempt you out. The fence is attainable but so far away. Hit the ball with the right grace and suddenly summoned power from your torso to your wrist, the big and the little rotating parts of you, something you never thought about as a kid, you just did it. You feel the concussion in the palm of your hand. It's the force of two young men fighting against each other in a battle sublimated to bat and ball, a barely symbolic struggle, a force strong enough to dent metal and split wood. The ball lifts high in the summer air toward the fence, and it may one day go over. For these are possible fences.

After practice, you chance Rt. 3 back. The parents don't like this since it is on the main road and more traffic. But it's the fastest way into and out of town. It takes you past the new building of the Gilster plant on the right, where Shredded Wheat cereal and marshmallows are made, past the bluff overlooking the old Death Row building and Menard Correctional Center below.

You ride into town past Hardee's, which you pass with just a thought—something better waiting for you at home. In the center of town, two blocks from your house, Rt. 3 makes its one zigzag in a 100 miles. Branching off it to the northeast, Rt. 150 heads into the interior of Illinois, toward towns like Sparta, Pinckneyville, Mount Vernon—rivals in baseball—and past the Chester Dairy Company which has been bottling the second best beverage in town since before the first horseless carriage could transport it, for almost a century.

Straight ahead, toward the river is the downtown, notably the old Chester Opera House, the VFW, then the Violence Prevention Center, Century 21, some buildings that look more like garages than offices, cheap storefronts, and Union shops where young men just out of high school learn the concept "paid what I'm worth." Their relation to money has changed.

To the north is The Dairy, to the south the biggest industry in town. It makes something to go with the milk. Its two large buildings made of town brick pretty much make up two whole blocks. It's one block from your house. Gilster Mary Lee, in fact, is as pleasantly named as the girl next door. She is the second largest employer in town and the best summer job you will ever have. Her five white silos are practically the only silos in the depressed farm community, operating at full capacity. You ride your bike in the shade between her buildings. Overhead and bridging the two buildings is a metal chute or ductwork conveyor, like a walking bridge slanted between Gilster buildings, connecting the warehouse on the south side of the street with the factory on the north. It looks so unadventitious in this quirky little town that it is impossible to tell which came first, the ductwork or the street that runs beneath it.

You ride across the shade of the chute laid like a finish line. Should a crack occur in that chute at high point of production, the whole town would be flooded with—cake mix. Gilster Mary Lee Corporation makes cake mix. Goes good with the milk.

Gilster Mary Lee: Should a crack occur in that chute at high point of production, the whole town would be flooded with—cake mix.

· · · · ·

The private label food manufacturing plant Gilster Mary Lee Corporation employs over 100 Chester residents and many from neighboring towns, offering both convenience and a sort of local pride to townsfolk who don't have to fight the fifty miles north to work at the big name Purina in St. Louis. Yes, one of the best summer jobs you'll ever have is working at a cake factory, and many Chester high schoolers find their first taste of factory work so satisfying that they never leave. After the prison system, Gilster is the best employer in town.

Chester, it's a hard town to leave.

You ride under the ductwork and rise over the handlebars to push yourself the final short block home. The corner of Light and Swanwick is as sharp as the brow of a ship, pointed toward the Mississippi. It's a corner so sharp it almost makes an angle, and a Turnpike Double missing the maze of Rt. 3 a block away must jackknife to make it.

You glide your bike into the small front yard and drop it on the lawn in front of the sturdy rough red brick, two-story home on the corner, under the one sufficient shade tree. The power company has had to amputate her street side limbs for the power lines. The flat brown roof of your home broods protectively and the French doors in the front let onto the *enclosed* porch addition, which was meant as no affront to the neighbors. You're at the center of town. You're home. The smell of yellow cornbread welcomes you.

Supper is the sound of your mom in the kitchen, and your mom is the sound of supper. You shower, eat meatloaf and cornbread, sponging butter and grape jelly 'till the sharp corners of the cube stain purple. You watch the Cardinals game on TV with your dad as the heat soaked in all day from the sun continues to rise off of your bare shoulders. You go to bed and say your prayers on the pillow.

Light and Swanwick is not a very peaceful place to sleep, especially on summer nights when you don't have air conditioning. All your windows upstairs are open, and all night the trucks are roaring a block away;

sometimes they enter your dreams as lions enter the dreams of African boys on the hot savannah, you imagine, the heat still rising off your chest. When your family finally gets a window unit, it only has enough cooling power for the living room—so you and your two brothers drag your sleeping bags downstairs to the one air-conditioned room. A block away, the main artery of southwestern Illinois cuts peremptorily through town and carries rude traffic. Shirtless on sleeping bags, legs restless, shadows spinning on the walls as a block away trucks drone on into the night all night you dream... of baseball. And a certain girl. And of baseball. You dream of dreams.

There are dreams beyond the fence, beyond the town. You dream of the Niagara roar from 30,000 fans filling Busch Stadium, and you tip your hat in brief acknowledgment of the crowd and betrayal of your modesty and round the bases, a feeling that can't be felt but once in a lifetime, if that. You glide around the bases, and a girl with her pretty fingers in the fence is watching, you know, and you come home where your best friends and the most courageous men you know greet you and pound you on the back. It is the feeling of the Great. It only comes with dreaming.

Far into the night trucks drone and interrupt dreams. Coal trucks roar warnings on empty streets, carrying loads of coal from the nearby mines to the docks south of Chester. She is a town exploiting her penultimate resource. Her final resource is her sons.

The sons of Chester, they have dreams. And they will follow them.

In the summer of 1993, a dream dawned on nine local boys. They came together with a dream. This is the story of chasing their dream. This is the story of the dream.

CHAPTER ONE
A Lot to Leave Chester

"Can't you do something about it?" said Sharon helplessly. The Monopoly game was getting louder. The Braun's next door might complain.

"They'll figure it out," Danny replied. "Someday." And he went back to his evening paper.

Sharon sighed. In 1974 Danny Ohlau, the quiet, unassuming three-sport star athlete at little Chester High, had fallen in love with the sweet, maroon bell-bottomed, God-fearing Catholic class secretary Sharon Bert. When Danny set school records in distance running and led Chester to its first ever regional basketball championship his senior year, his head swelled a bit, figuratively speaking. Sharon had to tell him: "I know you're good. You know you're good. Now let's just keep it to ourself." It was the first and last time Dan Ohlau ever bragged.

Danny went to college at SIU in Carbondale, the two married, and Danny got a good job offer in the big city fifty miles to the north, St. Louis. For a few days he struggled cruelly over whether to take it or stay in his hometown and accept the one job that paid best: the penitentiary.

It takes a lot to leave Chester. In the end, they stayed.

They bought a home three doors down from St. Mary's.

Three of the consequences of their decision now sat intently around the family game board: Jason, Craig who would become known as "Bobber," and Kurt. Jason looked the most like their father, including a slight gap in the front teeth, and even wore a fuzzy crewcut like his dad. Bobber's hair was almost silver and worn short like a helmet, with perfect hairline, as though his mother meant to have the barber make him look like Barbie's Ken. Kurt's hair was an O-Cedar mop of white blonde, as thick as thatch. The family poker and Monopoly games held religiously at the Ohlau's could quickly turn into all-out battles between the brothers. Today, the family feud was aggrandizing to world takeover. Bobber had landed on Park Place.

"You son of a—"

Danny dipped the paper just enough to show his frown. "*Jason.*"

Jason, the oldest, was the most like his dad. His eyes glowed with good humor but could flash a hint of meanness when necessary, especially if his little brothers challenged him. And they always challenged him.

"Mom, Bobber didn't pay me! He owes me fifteen hunnerd! I got Park Place, and I got a hotel."

One day Jason will own the Chester Dairy. His sense of real estate righteousness was early developed. His little brother had landed on Park Place.

Bobber smiled, displaying some of the imperturbable cool of his father and half the saintliness of his mother. "I don't have to pay you if you don't collect," he said, a reasonable plea for brotherly mercy. There lurked a keen conniving behind the brim of his Catholic halo. "Anyways, I'm not on the property anymore; I'm on Mom's." Bobber looked even more hopefully to his mother. "Mom, what do I owe you for Baltic? You've only got one apartment."

They all knew Mom was a soft heart when it came to just about anything. Especially money. "How about... five dollars," she said, the very opposite of begrudging.

"I can do that," Bobber quickly agreed.

"Bobber, if you don't pay me for Park Place, I'm gonna..." Bobber had seen his older brother grit his teeth that way on the baseball field.

"What are you gonna do? I don't owe you!"

"Yes, you do! *Dad*!"

Mr. Ohlau peeked over the top of the Sports Page. "For chrissake, we are not the Turners. If you guys wanna fight, go outside. If not, play the game." And from behind the ready curtain of the latest baseball box scores, he added, "And, Craig, if you land on a property, you have to pay."

Much different than his oldest son was laid-back second son Craig Robert. If Jason had a coil of aggressiveness that could spring at an opponent — namely his younger brothers, just to keep them in line — Bobber carried himself with an almost lazy comportment, relaxed but deceptive. The boy who never missed weekend Mass could also store up in a week plenty for Confession. There was a slight angle and asymmetry to his eyes, betraying as much cunning as Catechism. But if the two brothers differed in their composition, they shared an obsession for beating the other in competitions. They were born competitors, and when the competition got too fierce, the Braun's next door often had to put up with the overspill—arguments in the backyard, BB gun wars, and the like. Years later their father would sum things up: "They've struggled playing together from the age of one to the present day. Each one simply wanted to out-duel the other, no matter what it was that they were doing. Even in diapers."

But fight was not always a bad thing. It would prove to be the habit not only of brothers but of champions.

The Master of Park Place glared at the delinquent renter who maintained eyebrows of innocence, held high as if by a single stitch. Jason was a hotheaded, competitive bully who never wanted to lose to his younger brother, and often picked on him, flicking him behind the ear, throwing his tennis shoes out the car window. Bobber, of course, heaped on himself the jealous reaction of others, on purpose and by accident of his talent. He was always trying to beat his older brother, without the competition devolving to physical altercation, except for the time before school when he punched his big brother in the nose because his dad told him to if Jason ever messed with him again. Bobber struck when the soap was in his brother's eyes. Jason returned the favor—just as Bobber closed the frosted glass shower door like a shield. The star-shaped hole in the shower door is still there.

"Leave it there," said their dad.

To this day, the star-jagged hole in the shower door remains. Neither brother ever threw another punch.

As for their little brother Kurt, he could only watch his two older brothers and learn, what to do, what not to do. Kurt was tow-headed, always a burnished gold helmet of hair and a shade of freckles beneath his eyes and bridging the nose. Like any little brother, Kurt was greatly loved and, it is no contradiction, victimized. Brotherly abuse. He watched his older brothers with wonder and disengagement. Kurt was the innocent bystander, quiet, almost mysterious, in his thoughts.

But he could squeal when he felt trapped. He had just landed in Jail.

"Yooou be alright." His dad snapped his paper smooth and hid his face.

·   ·   ·   ·   ·

Laissez-faire was more than a disposition; it was the policy Danny Ohlau had acquiesced to at the prison job. Every weekday morning, he drove the short distance down the bluff to the penitentiary, parked his box-shaped Isuzu in a cramped, designated spot, and got himself penned in. Danny's job was to guard inmates. His boys never thought much about Menard, even though it held some of the worst criminals in the history of America. Their dad never talked about it. Yes, the little hometown of Chester, Illinois, held one of the highest concentrations of evildoers in the world.

Chester's outskirt held more murderers, serial killers, serial rapists, and child molesters than all the big cities in America combined.

But you never feared them. After all, your dad was keeping an eye on them. Him you feared. But you loved him much more than you feared him.

There was the time after a grade school basketball game. Bobber's team lost in overtime to county rival Sparta. Bobber hit a three to tie it up in regulation, then stupidly fouled out in overtime.

You don't know why he was pissed. It was because of something you did on the court, the way you played. Or maybe a bad day at work. Or to simply teach you a lesson about winning. You were always a "stubborn learner," he said. Must be because you were the middle son. You asked him where was mom and Kurt, and he said to you, "Oh, we're walkin' home tonight, son."

It was a cold, snowy night. You walked all the way home. All your buddies were driving by. Your house was a mile from the gym. You saw every crack in the sidewalk.

·   ·   ·   ·   ·

Bobber's development as an athlete was as much dependent on his relationship with his dad as on his genes. He remembers age five, throwing rocks into the Mississippi or into the creek on his grandfather's farm; at age seven, he and his brothers setting up what they deemed to be a world-class whiffle ball field on an open acre, complete with a backstop made from old screens and an outfield fence from old barn wood. To stop the arguments over balls and strikes, they rolled over a rusty burn barrel behind home plate. If the ball struck the barrel, the ping would umpire a strike. This was intended to prevent arguments. It rarely did. Bobber could make a whiffle ball sail through the air like magic and almost dent the barrel—or nick it just enough to pick a flake of rust off.

"Strike three!"

"Unh uh!"

When he was nine, Bobber and his father would play catch in the yard every evening, until the light got so dim Danny had to bring out a living room lamp so the game could continue. Bobber played Little League two years up with his brother and the eleven-year-olds. He was able to put any pitch from the mound right where he wanted it; he swung from the left side with an effortless swing that, in Chester at least, seemed to come around only once in a generation. On top of it all, he could run.

Though all the practice made him extremely efficient and heady when it came to the game, it couldn't make up for one problem. He never could throw as hard as the other dominant pitchers in the league. So he learned a curveball. His dad showed him the grip.

No matter how many coaches Bobber had over the years, he only really had one coach. His dad. In their championship runs in baseball, when he wasn't coaching, his dad would be standing with a couple other dads down the line. A Think Tank of dads. If mothers supplied food and unconditional moral support—their relative ignorance of the game an actual comfort to a boy—fathers supplied a mentality. Baseball calls on more wisdom than any other game. It's the pauses in the action. These are times to think. Some of the best thinking that is done at these times is in the form of clichés, the worn truths you rely on. You dig down to hold your ground. Wisdom is when a cliché suddenly rings personal. "Don't take your eyes off the ball." "Follow through." It was advice that won the war your grandpa fought in. It may have been football that prepared men for the attacks of battle, the sketching aforethought on map paper and the charge and fusillade, but the long waiting periods before, the concentration in the cockpit over enemy territory, the one-eye-clenched peering through a crosshairs—it was baseball that conditioned the mentality of American boys from Brooklyn to San Francisco for WWII. Eisenhower was a football player, leading surges of one army against another, but Ted Williams (after batting .406) flew a fighter plane, long waits and one moment to strike. Baseball was America's game.

Your dad taught you how to throw straight, and he taught you how to throw a curveball as his father before him had taught him. "Perfect. Just perfect," he'd say. *There were only two throws in your life you'd like back. One of them went through the neighbor's window. . .*

The truth was the boys never understood much of what their father was thinking. "Why doesn't he ever give us anything we want?" they asked each other. "Is it cuz we're poor?" When you are well loved you are never sure if you're poor.

What they wanted more than anything was their own *basketball* court, sort of like a man with land now wants to build a house. By the time Jason was ten and Bobber was eight, basketball had become their obsession. The Chicago Bulls games were regularly aired on Chester TV and both brothers fed on dreams of becoming the next Michael Jordan. They searched the town—arguing the whole time over who got to dribble the ball—for a convenient hoop. They begged their dad for an adjustable hoop on which they could begin the ascent to their highest, most inconceivable, ambition: dunking. About two white kids in Chester County could dunk. But their dad quietly denied them.

Then one day a big barrel of a truck backed up into their driveway off Swanwick, under the amputated tree. It must be some mistake. While Jason and Bobber watched with mouths half open, a sludge of muddy gray ice cream began to poop out the auger. By the end of the day, they had a backyard miracle: a 20' x 15' concrete slab, with a ten-foot basket.

"Michael Jordan doesn't play on a six-foot hoop," was all the explanation Danny would give. They didn't need any more.

There was no way their dad was going to rein in his sons' competitive drive. Only steer it slightly. Give it a platform. Thus, the concrete. Their dad had built his muscles and endurance on the local family farm. His mile record in high school would hold up 15 years. That backyard court, fenced in on three sides—not a bad metaphor for channeling the drive of cattle farmer sons.

They say the nuns of Seattle sometimes had to shut the windows of the Catholic school next door when the great John Stockton as a kid would battle against his older brother. In the east, the great college star Christian Laettner had likewise suffered a regular beating from his older brother. Great competitors all over the country are forged by the benign battle of brothers. In the Midwest, in little Chester, Illinois, the competition for backyard king of the court began, like the start of all wars, by the assertion of rights and fierce territorialization. Especially when you tried to go in for a layup. When Bobber fouled his brother, Jason fouled him back. The battles were fierce, but the blood was between brothers. Often there was shouting.

"Can't you do something about it?" Sharon sadly appealed to her husband. She was worried Father Dennis three doors down might hear.

Danny Ohlau barely shrugged. "They'll figure it out," he said. "Someday."

CHAPTER TWO
Blue Fog

The hot smell of movie beaming from the balcony projector filled the Chester Opera House. The silent film projectionist was Elzie, a wry and good-humored 18-year-old. He relaxed his arm, and the mesmerized crowd of 650 townsfolk suddenly came back to the real world. Mrs. Griffin at the player piano played on, sometimes threatening hymn, as the houselights were lit. Elzie, who could keep a good steady cranking going for a whole twenty-minute show and who sometimes played the tap drums for evening dances, took out a glass slide and a wax pencil. He started sketching a cartoon. Tonight it was Rocky Fiegel, the fist-flailing, toothless, chisel-bodied, corncob-pipe smoking local legend, "feared for his ability to render a good butt whooping even when attacked by several adversaries at once," as would be written of the local legend 90 years later. The young Elzie Segar cranked, and his caricature sketch flashed on the screen. Everybody laughed.

Elzie couldn't wait to get home. The ruts left by the milk wagons roughened his steps as he rushed the mile home to Old Plank Road. The letter had come all the way from Cleveland, Ohio: a correspondence course from W.L. Evans School of Cartooning and Caricaturing, "The School That has the Long Established Reputation." Mr. Schuchert, who owned the Opera House, had seen Elzie's talent often enough to pay for the course. And so, late into the night Elzie practiced his sketches, curling the pencil in his skillful grip, limning and shading. Funny, funnier, funniest—that was the goal. As Elzie Crisler Segar would reflect, years after he became famous, he literally "lit up the oil lamps about midnight and worked on the course until 3 a.m."

The year was 1912, and by the start of The Great War, Segar had finished the 20 lessons of the W. L. Evans System, roughly one dollar a lesson. He would make nearly half a million a year during the Depression off his cartoon drawings. Elzie Crisler Segar's creations would be known the world over.

After leaving Chester, Segar never returned. Lured by the big city, he created eight cartoons for the Chicago sports pages while covering the infamous 1919 World's Series; then on to New York where "the day I arrived in the big town," as he put it, he began creating a new cast of characters. One of the characters was named for the locally made product that had first put Chester on the map in the 19th century: Castor Oyl. When Castor's daughter, Olive, needed a boyfriend, Segar had a stroke of genius and created, in his own words, "a funny-looking old salt down by the docks." The character would become one of the iconic characters of the 20th century: Popeye the Sailor Man. Somehow growing up in Chester, Illinois, 500 miles from the nearest sailor's port, Segar had come up with a caricature that would become the most famous sailor in the world. Chester folks recognized it immediately. It was Rocky Fiegel.

The real-life Popeye, Chester's Frank "Rocky" Fiegel from early 20th century

Many of Mr. Segar's immortal characters, of course, are based on the people of Chester. Olive Oyl was based on turn-of-the-century Chester general store owner, the tall, thin Dora Paskel; Wimpy ("I will gladly pay you Tuesday...") after Segar's boss, Bill Schuchert. People living in Chester today can trace their ancestry to a cartoon character.

You know these characters. They're your friends, the great-grandchildren of Popeye and Bluto and Olive Oyl and Wimpy. You know their antics and character: the tough guy bully, the Yorkshire forearm, the haymaker punch, the squeaky heart-throbbing, love-struck girlfriend, and of course Popeye, the goofy, muttering, doughty, indefatigable underdog who redefined the depths of comeback.

Elzie Segar working on cartoons in his studio

To this day, Chester harbors a collection of characters. Small towns do that. Just as certainly as the open ranges of Montana attract and, mutually, create a kind of personality, or the buzz and bright lights of New York City lure and make her eclectic citizenry, so too the southern Illinois way of life on the banks of the Mississippi River beckons and breeds a certain type. *Character*—not a moral quality but an idiosyncrasy that might not be mistaken for psychological pathology on her neighborly streets, in her family-owned stores and bars, on her front porches. There was the sports card shop owner where the boys traded cards by the Dime

Store who would go through all the packs and take out the star athletes before he sold the packs to kids. There was the town drunk who taught Catechism with all the good cheer of an Irish pub owner addicted to his wares, easily accessing one cup and another. There was the junior high coach who complained to his benchwarmers in a huddle after the final buzzer, "Some of you aren't getting into the game 'til it's literally over." There was the cross country coach, so heavy set he could hardly walk; the high school basketball coach who got fired for punching a parent; the coach who regularly tempted God, pointing to the heavens, "Strike me down, if I'm lyin'" — then waited as the lightning bolt didn't come. *God sure is mercy*, Bobber thought.

There were bullies like Meat and Peters, the first among Bobber's cohorts to reach puberty, two of the biggest meanest boys of their age in the county. Adam Gibbs, nicknamed Meat, did his own thing with a bulldog attitude that was hard to question, if you wanted to keep your lips unbloodied. He was bigger than the rest of the boys and scared of no one.

There was the time he stood up to The Sheriff ... You'll never forget that.

The two, Peters and Meat, would become the physical backbone of the baseball team that would become a Chester legend, something that might be told to grandchildren someday.

Swanwick Street itself had its own cast of characters. There was old cat-eyed Mrs. Robinson, two houses down from the Ohlau's, who couldn't recognize her own grandniece through a screen door but seemed to know all the neighbors' business. It was a typical town vigilance that could easily be mistaken for a busybody, but is better accepted than criticized. It may save your life to have someone watching over you. Just as, as Lincoln once rhapsodized, a foreign army could never take a single sip from a tributary of the Mississippi, neither could a single foreign spy get past Mrs. Robinson. If someone from Red Bud tried to sneak into town, Mrs. Robinson alerted a neighbor. Red Bud is just twenty miles up the road. Not minding your own business is a matter of town security.

Next door to the Ohlau's lived the Braun's. Jim was a Gilster Mary Lee mechanic who walked the one brief block to work each day in 87 strides, and Betty was a grocery store clerk who sat on the porch swing every night in good weather. Small town neighbor means proximity, means accepting the spillover from next door and the semi-permeable boundaries between homes and property, where the pink pompoms of peonies might mark a border line or, for boys, an out of bounds. The Braun's hated the Ohlau boys and at the same time loved them. Anyone from a small town understands this.

The Taylors, an elderly couple in their 70's had moved close by the Ohlau's. Their love for each other and for others was long gone. Theirs was not a marriage but a bond of inured bitterness. They had only each other — and that was worse than nothing.

"Keep those damn balls from coming over here!" a raspy Mrs. Taylor would yell when the Ohlau balls went beyond the fence. "We're gonna call the cops on you boys!"

But bombardment by balls was not a local offense. It was a local tradition and a boy's prerogative. Balls were to be as put up with as bad weather and sports as anticipated as the seasons. Attendance at St. Mary's was hardly more consistent than Friday night football at W.O. Smith Field. Only one was optional.

. . . . .

If in Chester you had five hundred parents and aunts and uncles to watch over you and a thousand big brothers and sisters to rat on you, there was a freedom in the boundaries. The small-town vigilances and observances were generational traditions, and one's territory was guarded as though many acts of sacrifice and heroism had won your right to a home and a lawn. Nobody ever talked about the legends of fighting Injuns for this hill nor about the great Castor Oil Company built here that made Chester first thrive on the banks of the great river. High school football championships were what built this town. The wars were symbolic. A turf a hundred yards long and forty yards wide had been designated for battle. Banners were hung from the holy gym rafters to memorialize the victors.

Thus, Chester provided everything a boy could need growing up. Safe and quiet streets with enough traffic flow to keep things interesting, a neighbor or family member or friend behind virtually every screened porch, a court or playing field on every block, in every neighborhood a convenient apple or cherry or pear or plain old tree for climbing or a good hill for sledding in the winter, decent schools with classmates against whom you had a fair chance, close-knit townspeople who would not think but wave to you when you passed and inquire about your grandma's arthritis when they saw you at the Dime Store. Your life was always intersecting and, in some real sense, bound up with their own.

The town that offered a man a decent wage offered the boy the daily challenge of finding something to do. Or, for the more inventive type, the challenge of *making* something happen in a town where nothing ever much did. The river had once in a hundred years exceeded its banks, the prisoners—not a one had ever really escaped. It was up to you to make things happen.

Sometimes plans backfired, and from time to time the Ohlau boys found themselves in what is known as "a situation."

"BOBBER, COME DOWNSTAIRS RIGHT NOW."

One unusually cool June afternoon in the summer of 1991 that command came from the ground floor. The command of a correction officer at one of America's toughest prisons is not to be disregarded. The fact that the officer is also your father made it absolutely unrefusable. For a second, Bobber thought about maybe just pretending he didn't hear his name—or possibly even making a run for it.

The trouble had begun two hours earlier when he was walking through uptown Chester with his brothers Jason, eleven, and Kurt, who was six at the time.

It was a beautiful, early June day, with the sun high in the still cool summer sky. Air conditioners were not humming; windows all over town were open. The boys could've ridden bikes, gone to the courts, played mini golf or whiffle ball in the backyard, organized a game of baseball at St. Mary's Bowl, or even traded baseball cards at the card shop a block away—for they still needed the rookie cards of Bo Jackson and Ken Griffey, Jr.

Instead, on their trip uptown, they decided on going to a place where they had gone many times before to satisfy the insatiable passions of a boy: the Dime Store. It is almost too good to be true that you could buy a handful of anything you needed for close to a quarter. Candy bars, Candy Cigarettes, Soda (your mom wouldn't let you drink it), three whiffle balls, a small bottle of Brute, Firecrackers, and what was even better, Smoke Bombs. Everything *seemingly* dangerous. The smoke bombs were even better than the Cigarettes. The smoke bombs—you could actually light them. The Ohlau brothers exited the store with a bag full of them and three quarters to spare.

On the way home there seemed only one perfect target: the Taylor's. The mean old couple had moved in across the street a year ago. Their old house and shaky fence and unkempt lawn seemed to invite a little excitement.

"You go hold the backdoor for us," Jason told their little brother. Kurt obediently ran to his spot and stationed himself as obediently as a getaway car driver.

Jason and Bobber leaned against the rough bark of an elm tree as they had seen soldiers do in war movies. Jason lit a smoke bomb, rolled away from the tree, and fired a fastball in the direction of the Taylor's fence. "Dang, it's not going to make it," he said.

Ricocheting off the dirty whitewashed fence, the

bomb took two bounces and came to a stop in the middle of the sidewalk. The boys watched from behind a tree as red smoke rose like a genie.

"Let's go home," Bobber said as the bomb fizzled.

"Like hell we're going home. You try it."

After seeing his older brother fail at something he thought would be so easy to do, Bobber agreed. "I'll do you one better though. Instead of getting it over the fence, I'll get it in the window," referring to the open first-floor window ten feet behind the fence.

"What?" Jason replied. "The window?" "Yeah... . . the open window, right over there," Bobber answered, pointing. "Do you know how much shit we could get in for that?" Jason laughed. "You can't do it anyway,"

"Like hell I can't," Bobber reluctantly replied. The skinny, soon to be 4th grader reached into his small brown sack and selected the blue bomb. Blue was his favorite color. He fondled the sandy roughness in his fingers as he would a curveball. Jason lit the wick.

"We're leaving as soon as I throw it," he told his big brother, spying his target. "We can't get caught doing this. We could get into some deep shit."

With his left-handed windup, he heaved the sparkling ball of potassium chlorate directly at the house. It went over the fence and through the overgrown oak branches guarding half the house.

"H o l y shit," said Jason. "It went in the freakin'

window!"

The brothers paused in disbelief. Rich blue smoke was coiling its way out of the open first-floor window. Then angry screams fumed from the house. The Taylor's sounded like they were as mad at each other as at the smoke.

"Let's get the hell out of here!"

The boys made it to their back door breathing excitedly. Kurt had the door open.

Peeking out the kitchen window curtain, a clear view to the front of the Taylor's, they saw the old man and woman standing outside, clearly distraught. Gesticulating at their open window, blue fog still dissipating, the old couple's fear was turning into anger.

From the safety of the kitchen, Jason whispered, "We made it"—but with a sense of incomplete escape.

Just as the boys began to feel they had gotten away scot-free, a glimpse of another old figure came into view. Slowly walking up Light Street, and repeatedly pointing in the direction of the boys' house like she was trying to poke a thread through a needle, was old Mrs. Robinson.

"Crap," said Jason and Bobber at the same time.

Mrs. Robinson stood with the Taylors for approximately fifteen minutes, over and over describing to her neighbors exactly what she saw—and even sort of winding up in imitation of the pitch. Witness for the prosecution.

You got to be kidding me, Bobber thought to himself. *No way did she see me throw that.*

"She can barely see two feet in front of her face, no way she seen us," Jason said. Then he turned to his brother and looked him right in the eyes. "We're going to deny everything."

. . . . .

It wasn't until around 4:30 p.m. that their Corrections Officer dad arrived home from the maximum security prison. The three Ohlau boys were unusually well behaved, having absconded to the upstairs. Five minutes after their father walked into the house a knock sounded on the front door. An unusually loud knock.

It was the police. Apparently, Mrs. Robinson had her glasses on. She had sworn up and down to the cop that she saw one of Danny's boys throw a smoke bomb into the Taylor's living room window.

"The left-handed one."

"BOBBER, COME DOWNSTAIRS RIGHT NOW!"

The cop, a 300-pound, 20-year veteran of the Chester police force, towered over the 80-pound boy.

Trying to hide his nervousness, Bobber stood hardly able to breathe in front of the burly sergeant. Many words came out of the policeman's mouth, but the only thing that mattered to Bobber was when he heard him mention, "You know, young man, if I find out you did this, there is good chance you could be sent to the juvenile detention center and not able to attend school this year."

Bobber felt like he had just been gutted.

Was he serious? Bobber tried to discern, his thoughts starting to make him dizzy. *It was a total accident?* he wanted to plead. *Or was it?* There Bobber stood, heart pounding and mind racing about what he was going to say next. Although taught to *never* lie and knowing Catholic consequences for the great sin he was about to commit, he decided there was only one thing left to say. He put a stitch in his eyebrow to hold it up:

"Someone threw a smoke bomb?"

He had summoned his greatest innocence. "That is a shame that anyone would do such a thing, the Taylors are such nice people." That last part was the biggest lie of all.

The nine-year-old Bobber knew there was a good chance that neither his father nor the sergeant believed a word that had stumbled out of his mouth. But he wasn't going to juvie over a stupid smoke bomb. Besides, in the boys' minds, the Taylors, in some way, deserved it.

After everything was said, there was nothing the sergeant could do. All he had was the accusation of a half-blind old woman versus the denial of an innocent-eyed nine-year-old.

As the officer left the house, Bobber felt the relief fill him like new life, and he let out an audible wheeze.

"I don't know why you are so relieved," his father said as Bobber began to bound up the stairs. "If you didn't do it, you should have had nothing to worry about." The words made it almost impossible to take another step. "Now go get your brothers and get your shoes. There's work to do at the farm."

CHAPTER THREE
The Brothers and the Birth of a Dream

In a town the size of Chester the smoke bomb incident, naturally, created a bit of a buzz. Long after the innocuous blue smoke had cleared, people were still talking about it. And the Taylor's were still coughing. And cursing. The complaints and speculations, in fact, went on for a month and betrayed the fact that people in a small town are as interested in your life as you are — and that goes for the good and the bad. At the Main Street Café it was chuckled about over coffee by farmers who had come in from the field. At the bars it was slung around for want of a new local news story. Even at the penitentiary a few of the prisoners had somehow heard of it, and Danny Ohlau was left shaking his head in mute denial. He *should* have sent his sons to juvie.

In the main office at Chester Grade School, 30-year-old Tim Lochead, the hard-working, fair-minded grade school principal, heard about it. He had seen a lot in his short career as a teacher and administrator. Mr. Lochead looked a little bit like their own father, the slight gap in the front teeth that seemed to be a phenotypic trait among many of the townsmen, and his quick humor. He always wore a crisp white long-sleeved shirt and well-knotted tie.

He had dealt with students who were troublemakers, teachers who were lazy or incompetent or both and even with bachelor coaches accused of inviting female students over for dinner. He didn't tolerate much. However, the notorious summer incident, which he overheard his secretary speaking about, was a new one even on him.

The week before the start of school, on the morning of August 12, 1991, the young principal overheard Ms. Melissa Kyle, new third-grade teacher ask his secretary, "Did you hear about that Bobber kid? Threw the smoke bomb into the window of that house."

"I did hear about that. Almost caught the house on fire." That is the way all rumors are born and fanned.

Mr. Lochead had heard the story many times over, each time a variation on the central truth. A nine-year-old had thrown a lit smoke bomb through a six inch opening in a window from a hundred feet away. *Quite an arm*, he thought to himself, for he had been a baseball player himself. In one version, the house caught fire and burned to the ground. This rumor stood less certainly than the Taylor's old home, of course. Then there was the rumor that Bobber and his older brother would not be attending school on time this year because of confinement to a juvenile detention center. Some said that it wasn't Bobber who threw the bomb. It was Jason. It didn't matter to the young principal what version of the story was true or not. He just didn't want events like this ever happening at or around his school.

It was a new day, the first day of school, August 19,

1991, a day with nines and ones, a day friends come together, and the boy Bobber was certainly in attendance. Doc and Herb, the most popular boys in the school, were two of Bobber's closest friends. They were coming off a summer where most of their time had been spent playing baseball, riding bikes, and swimming in the community pool. Doc—his real name was Matt Davitz, thus MD—was a stocky, big-hearted, self-proclaimed "ladies man," who on occasion made ten-year-old girlfriends whisper among themselves. He was precocious in body with a bullet-shaped head and wore Elton John glasses that did something noteworthy when the sun came out: they turned into shades. The Chester school district had conferred upon him, the label "Gifted," which trait he often proved in both the classroom and the playground, and though his dad was but a Gilster lead man, it would not surprise anyone if his son did become a doctor.

Herb—his real name was Matt Seymour (no one, it seemed, could be properly dubbed at birth)—was an aspiring bodybuilder who ate nothing but chicken for dinner, for the protein, and popsicles for breakfast, for the sugar. This dietary discipline seemed to have some effect. He was short but stocky of frame. His fiery disposition seemed the perfect complement to Bobber's cool and easy demeanor.

The three boys were extremely close, nearly inseparable on a given summer day. "If we are always going to hangout we need a cool name for our group," the three decided that first day of school. "And it can't be some lame name either."

The very next day as the first-hour bell rang, Herb came running up, late for school. He had a name for the group: *The Smothers Brothers*.

Now, Herb had no idea who the actual Smothers Brothers were or what they stood for, but the name was a quirky rhyme. "Smothers" was funny; "Brothers" was true and cool. The real Smothers Brothers, from the 60s, were often on TV performing a trademark comedy act of folk songs and humor with contrived arguments between the two. The brothers' comedy was cleverly critical of the political mainstream–"Ronald Reagan is a known heterosexual" —and their sympathetic stance toward the emerging movements, anti-war, civil rights, and counterculture, made them likeably controversial.

The Smothers Brothers it was. The Smothers Brothers of small-town Chester were an elite group. The Brothers limited the group to only a few lucky members. In order to be accepted into the fraternity, a kid had to meet specific qualifications.

First, and extremely important for athletic development, no girls allowed.

Second, the boy had to be fast. Fast enough to almost beat Bobber in a race.

Third, he had to be able to throw a Turbo whistler football with extreme accuracy and enough distance to travel the length of the blacktop in front of the school.

Fourth, he had to be able to make a three-point shot with a basketball on a ten-foot rim.

Lastly, he had to be an overall "cool" fourth grader.

None of these were thought to be in the least subjective. Either you were cool, or you couldn't throw a ball.

Not too many kids in the class met the qualifications needed for the club, but every now and then, one deserving prospect would arise, or a potential talent would make his application.

Applications were received weekly. Once enough applications were received (three to five was usually the number), a tryout would be held. Taking the interested applicants to the playground during recess time, The Brothers would put them through a vigorous workout, similar to that of a professional team tryout, and rate them in five crucial categories:

1. *Fast Speed* 1 2 3 4 5
2. *Football Throw* 1 2 3 4 5
3. *Arm Restling* 1 2 3 4 5
4. *Three frows in 1 minute* _____
5. *Cool* 1 2 3 4 5

The tryout criteria proved to be too much for many of the applicants. In its first year of existence, the group failed to add a single new member. But as the summer of 1992 began, The Brothers, now headed to fifth grade, were still looking to add a couple new faces. Three boys, Mike Niermann, Zach Engel, and James Knott, had made strides in recent months and were among the potential prospects.

The boys knew Zach and James from school. Zach

had a pool, a satellite, a big screen TV, and most importantly, an adjustable basketball hoop. These assets elicited profound consideration for membership. His dad, Floyd, was a barge operator and beer drinking town legend who harbored stashes of dynamite, guns, and booze. These assets too were positively viewed. James was as nice as a friend could be, loyal to a fault, especially when it meant protecting a brother from trouble. His dad, Dale, was a mental health center technician. He was comparable to Zach's dad in that neither had any problem putting down a 30 pack of suds in one sitting. These were admirable, pseudo-athletic skills that the boys could not help but think highly of. But there would come the day when The Brothers realized something. Their Brother hated the fact that his father was an alcoholic. Four of The Brothers were at his house one day to swim and play hoops. They ended up pouring out 20 beers ceremoniously into the woods behind his house. They all watched as the golden foam soaked back into the ground like a demon disappearing from Middle Earth.

There was one other boy, Mike Niermann, big boned, tall and athletic, who seemed worthy of membership. But there was a problem. He attended the Catholic school. Did they really want a parochial school kid in their club? These boys must be held in constant suspicion. For they may know something you don't …

But Mike was too good to pass on. He had good athleticism and could hold his own against Doc in "arm restling."

After inducting the new members, the club was now complete. Six well-qualified members: Bobber, Matt "Doc" Davitz, Matt "Herb" Seymour, James "Rainman" Knott, Mike Niermann, and Zach Engel. In total they brought to the playground, of whatever kind, all virtues necessary. Bobber was the most athletic, a quiet leader by example; Doc the vocal leader and liaison (if necessary) to the girls (should that would be needed); Herb with the short bodybuilder physique was disciplined and tough—he had boxed his twelve-year-old brother when he was seven, and when his brother nearly knocked out his tooth, he kept punching, blood pouring out of his mouth and off his chin; the tooth turned black and stayed that way for years; Mike was tall and athletic and proved that even though he was a parochial school kid, he could fit in. After all, he was the right socio-economic class: his mom was a cafeteria cook, and his dad, a Gilster Mary Lee mechanic. Zach was the rich kid of the group, with the rare amenities of recreation, pool, big screen, and adjustable hoop. James was rail thin, a very nice kid who listened to classic rock constantly, the Steve Miller Band, AC/DC, Bad Company. When James shot threes on the outdoor hoops, his arch was so high he brought rain, the boys bragged, thus "Rainman." Just as a machine consists of several key parts, the six together filled almost every slot physically, mentally, and spiritually (the parochial kid not to be despised after all). Together they would become a near perfect team.

Over the years, Mr. Lochead's mirrory profile could

be seen in the Principal's Office window as he kept an eye on The Brothers playing and roughhousing on the playground. *We haven't seen anything like that around here in a while*, he would nod to himself, after watching Bobber throw a ball all the way from the outfield home, then turn back to the window. *Ever.*

The six started the summer of 1993, between fifth and sixth grade, with two goals in mind. The first goal was sought after without saying: to have as much fun as possible. The second goal was more elusive. A dream. But it had come to them — no one later would be able to remember how. Perhaps that is how all dreams come, as ghosts come, sliding into habitations, entering imaginations. The goal was simple but hard. It came to them as they played and argued and tamped the dust at the bottom of St. Mary's Bowl. It came to them at sleepovers, ironically named for no one ever slept, as they lay bare-chested on the thin mattress of open sleeping bags on hard living room floors and talked late into the night of things so honest and hidden they had never even whispered them aloud. The dream came to them. It was to win the Class "A" Khoury League Championship in baseball. The National Championship.

No one from Chester had ever dreamed that before.

PART TWO: CHAMPIONS

CHAPTER FOUR
The Blitzkrieg

George M. Khoury founded what is known as the Khoury League in 1934. The program he started expanded rapidly after World War II, first in the regions close to the inaugural city of St. Louis, then to Illinois, Kentucky, Florida, and other states. This national program was the first of its kind. It shepherded kids out of the sandlot and into organized youth baseball all over the country. The league also pioneered post-season playoffs for teams of equal standing in their respective division — Atoms, Bantams, Midgets, and Juveniles — with the different classes A, B, C, and D, designating how a team had finished in the regular season.

Chester had no history of involvement in the Khoury League. It had been the dream of every generation of boys in and around the city of St. Louis to advance to and win the Class "A" National Baseball Tournament. This dream didn't dawn on the sons of Chester until the summer of 1993. The area of southern Illinois, always abuzz with St. Louis Cardinal broadcasts, every evening emanating like sonar from living room TVs and front porch radios, afternoon games blaring from the cabs of tractors in the field from spring planting to the fall harvest. Nothing kept a wide community more in tune than a Cardinals baseball game, as much a part of a summer evening as Country Western or Rock and a stool at the Main Street Tavern, or a porch swing and a freshly poured glass of sweet tea. Now Chester had something as a precursor. Now they had the Khoury League.

"Boys, this calls for a celebration!" Doc announced as he caught his glove and found his baseball cap near the mound. The tossing of the gloves and the whipping off of hats and frisbeeing them in the air and the dog pile and the hugs and high fives cannot even be practiced. These celebrations of victory cannot even be pretended.

On the hot summer evening of July 8, 1993, the Chester Midget 1 baseball team with all six Brothers in the lineup held a genuine celebration on Cohen Field. They had just finished beating one of their biggest rivals, the club from nearby Marissa, another group of eleven-year-olds with elastic lined uniform tops and mid-calf pants, the best team from the neighboring county where baseball too was treated as a sacred tradition. With the win, the Midgets secured a Class "A" playoff berth. A celebration was in definite order.

Mike said his mom was making chicken and dumplings and it was a big pot.

"Mike's!" they unanimously agreed. Bobber, Doc, Herb, Rainman, and Zach rushed home, grabbed some clothes and magazines and blankets and candy bars and any other "supplies" needed for a sleepover at the Niermann's. But sleep was the last thing on their minds.

The creamy smell of chicken 'n dumplings drew the champions of Class A through the screened in front door of the Niermann house where they encountered Mike's dad, Joe. An inveterate joker, he winked and threw an inside curveball in the direction of the group, specifically at Bobber and Doc. "Now you two guys better not order any Pam Anderson on the satellite tonight," he winked.

"We won't, Joe," replied Doc, smiling sheepishly. "We learned our lesson."

Just a month before, at the home of Doc's loving aunt, the two delinquents let their boyish curiosities, not yet risen to the level of craving, get the best of them.

After sitting down in the living room at the end of a hard day of play, the two had decided to flip on the satellite. After sifting through the potential viewing options, the two came to a fair option. How about a cartoon? "Let's turn it on the channel with the bunny," Doc suggested. He had heard that was a good channel.

"Sounds good to me," Bobber replied, and they sat back with a Snickers bar apiece to watch.

Turns out, they had bitten off more than they could chew.

"*The Best of Pamela Anderson*," read the channel box as a picture appeared. "This has to be good," thought Bobber, sitting up. It was no cartoon.

"She's that girl from *Baywatch*, right?" said Doc.

"I think so—." Bobber suddenly jumped up, realizing something. "It's not free! It costs like thirty bucks!"

But Doc hit "Enter." "I can't think of a better way to spend thirty bucks," he said. "Anyways, my aunt will never know we ordered it."

And that simply, the boys Entered a world they

barely knew existed.

But there was a price to pay for adult indiscretions, especially if you're a boy. Turns out, people get monthly bills for such purchases....

Learning from their past mistake, the boys planned nothing of the sort for this night. The six friends sat in Mike's basement trying to figure out what to do on the balmy, summer evening, the glory of their championship sitting in their souls like the satisfaction of a good meal. Mrs. Neirmann's chicken 'n dumplings could win a championship, Bobber had politely told Mike's mom. The boys picnicked their blankets on the indoor/outdoor carpet of the Neirmann basement floor and stretched out as satisfied as men smoking victory cigars. But victory was never so sweet as brotherhood. All they could talk about was baseball, and each had his moment. Mike and his home run. Bobber and his intentional plunking of Marissa's three-hitter. Zach's double in the gap. James making a diving play at second. Herb's leadoff triple in the seventh. But especially Doc putting the hard tag on the cleanup hitter at first—almost causing a bench-clearing brawl. The Midgets had never had a bench-clearing brawl and wouldn't that have been great!

The six talked until around nine o'clock and then decided on what they wanted to do. The video store uptown closed at ten, and if they wanted to rent a movie, they were going to have to hurry. They asked Linda, Mike's mom, if she could drive them. She agreed.

Knowing they weren't going to be able to rent the

tantalizing skin flicks that Chester Video kept on the side shelf—*Sliver, Sleep Away Camp*, or *Oh Calcutta*—the group instead would go with the next best thing: *WrestleMania VII*. For they had conquest in their blood.

As huge Hulk Hogan fans, they loved the old school, professional wrestling, which featured stars such as Andre the Giant, The Ultimate Warrior, Ric Flair, The Rockers, and their all-time favorite, The Hulkster. Hulkamaniacs without limit, the boys were thrilled to have the chance to watch the Hulk vs. Sgt. Slaughter in the main event. Thus the night was nicely scheduled, and Linda let them get some licorice to go with the movie. They also knew what, after a long and enjoyable boys' night, the morning was going to bring.

Earlier in the evening, Bobber informed the group that Micah, a friend of his older brother, had come across a stash of fireworks. *Fireworks*. The mere mention triggered the kind of excitement only a boy who has had no true brush with danger can feel—that is, danger without the danger. In Bobber, the Taylor incident of the summer before flushed up like embarrassment—and possibility. This admirable Micah was able to get his hands on twenty bundles of Bottle Rockets, six packs of M-100s, two packs of Roman Candles, and a cache of Saturn Missiles. This news was joy to their young mischievous ears. Not even Pamela Anderson was more interesting.

WrestleMania VII ended, and then ended again and again as with encore of devils that keep rising groggily from the dead, until the great Hulk, savior of the wrestling world, put a final stop to it with a sleeper hold. But sleep was hard to come by that night for the boys, with the impending excitement of the next day jitterbugging around in their heads.

The morning came with the sweet smell of hotcakes filling the Niermann house. The boys resurrected from the burial wraps of their blankets and sprang up the stairs. Linda was famous for her Gilster pancakes. She had worked for years in the cafeteria at the parochial school and knew how to turn a cake mix into a breakfast whose memory you could summon up in your nostrils for the rest of your life.

When the last of the maple syrup was smeared on the plate, the group asked to be excused from the table. They had plans. Bobber asked if he could use the phone and called his brother. The conversation was hushed and serious. Almost military-like. Bobber grilled Jason to see if he had talked with Micah. Yes, he had. A bottle rocket war was being planned in the Reiman's woods later that day.

Teams had already been formed. It was going to be Jason and Micah's crew vs. the Smothers Brothers. The six boys, although each much smaller than the boys two years ahead in school, never shied away from a challenge, especially when it involved fireworks. Weapons were great equalizers. The Brothers felt the inertia of their baseball championship and the fuel of Mrs. Neirmann's pancakes. Nothing seemed to be able to stop them.

Before setting off on the mile walk to Micah's, the

boys made last minute preparations for battle. They cut PVC pipes for guns, outfitted themselves with mantles of their dad's old hunting camouflage, and borrowed some of Joe's safety glasses for eye protection. The boys were knowledgeable of the safety procedures for combat of this type. They tried on the goggles with the savvy and care of a Sopwith Camel pilot. Although not exactly like the BB gun wars they were used to, bottle rocket wars required similar prophylaxis and discretion.

In a noble gesture to fairness and under an initial, sane obeisance to rules of the game, each team would be given an equal amount of fireworks. Ten bundles of bottle rockets, three packs of M 100's, one pack of Roman candles, and three Saturn missiles were divided between the militaries of five soldiers. Forts were assembled out of trees and brush, and the weaponry readied. The rules were set forth:

1. Bottle rockets can be fired at any time at anyone.

2. The thrower of any M100 must yell "incoming" before throwing an M100 into the opposing team's camp (that was only fair).

3. Similarly, each team had to provide warning before firing any Roman candle into the opposing team's camp.

And lastly,

4. If you get hit, you must sit out. (No one seemed to ever follow this one.)

"Incoming!" The loud blast of an M100 landing at Herb's feet marked the beginning of the most epic bottle rocket war the Reiman woods had ever suffered.

The older team, which consisted of Jason, Micah, and four other goons from the seventh-grade class, held nothing back. Advantages they held in testosterone they also secretly held in ammunition. They barraged the younger brothers with salvos of M100s and screaming Saturn missiles. Guarding against burns, the loss of a finger or eye or ear—or pride—The Smothers Brothers remained in tight cover behind the felled and rotting tree that had spent its own life to become their home base.

Following the initial one-sided assault, the youngsters fought back. They twisted bundles of rockets together and fired them in the direction of the goons. It seemed as if this strategy was working, as many rockets appeared to be making direct hits. However, rule four was going unheeded—shell shock amnesia, no player had yet to sit out. It was starting to look as though this battle was going to last until one team either gave up or ran out of ammunition.

About thirty minutes into the action, the pops of the rockets had slowed for the goons. The Brothers reckoned that if they were going to take any glory from the battlefield on this day, they would to have to do something bold.

Doc was always thinking. He called for a huddle behind the dark oak and presented the idea of twisting the remaining M100s into bundles of three, lighting them, and tossing them into the lap of the enemy.

"This will draw 'em out of the fort." Or so Doc estimated. "After they're in the open, let's hit 'em with everything we got."

The younger camp inventoried their remaining arsenal. Six Roman candles, three missile boxes, and a couple rockets. Doc and Mike would light the M100s and missiles, Bobber and James would do double barrel Roman Candles, and Herb and Zach would light the remaining rockets.

"Incoming!" "Incoming!" "Incoming!" shouted the boys in three waves.

For a whole eternal minute the woods turned into a thunder and lightning show, a microcosm of the great battles they had heard of—Gettysburg, Battle of the Bulge, even Vietnam. The loud bangs of the M100s rang out as bottle rockets hissed past the trunks of the sturdy oaks. The fireballs from the Roman Candles sparkled through the air, zeroing in on their targets. The screaming of the Saturn missiles muffled the screams of anger from the goons' fortress.

As the last rockets popped, the smoke-filled canopy of the enemy camp seemed to simmer with anger. Shock and outrage uglified the faces of Micah, Jason, and the goons. The Brothers looked at each other and knew what they had to do next.

"Run!" Bobber shouted.

With that, the six Brothers leaped over downed trees, pushed through troves of brush like wild Arkansas hogs, and sprinted out of the woods, the older boys tearing after them.

Reaching the entrance to Cole Park, a half mile from where their retreat began, The Brothers figured they had made it. They collapsed together on the grass and laughed.

After a minute of diaphragmatic paroxysms, a realization settled in. "You know those guys are pissed right?" said Herb, as if articulating the danger might make it more manageable. "And they'll probably get us back for this."

Unconcerned with such possibilities, the rest of the group continued celebrating the victory with high fives and whistling reenactments of the battle.

Beating the goons at their own game was a confirmation of sorts. This group of fifth graders wasn't going to back down from anybody in the future. If Jason and Micah's crew countered with something as payback for the loss they suffered on this day, The Brothers would be prepared and deal with it like men. After all, they were champions of the Midget League.

CHAPTER FIVE
The Merger

Baseball is not about just one thing. It's about combinations of things. Played at the highest level, it's about the order of the lineup, about communication between the pitcher and catcher, secret signals between batter and the coach down the third base line wiping his sleeve, the double play. Baseball is a game so precisely evolved that move second base one inch south, and the close play is a mere coincidence. Move home plate backward or forward, and the slider is no longer possible. Only lawn croquet has so many fixed points that must not be trifled with or all is lost.

As the young boys matured and as the years carried on, their dream of capturing the Class "A" National Championship in the Khoury League baseball tournament seemed more elusive than ever. There was one essential thing that they were lacking …

It was a meeting that took place every weekday. Each morning around 7:20 a.m. as Danny Ohlau pulled into the Menard Correctional Center lot, another familiar face was arriving. Gary Knop, one of the wardens, was a longtime friend who usually entered through the gates at about the same time as Danny. Usually, they would talk about baseball and their sons.

Talk over their frustrations—how Danny's Midgets had lost at state or how Gary's Juveniles, the next older group, couldn't get past districts. On this day, August 2, 1994, the conversation, as they stepped over the threshold, past the all-seeing "Electric Eye," and into one of the state's most dangerous prisons, took a slightly different turn.

As they made their way through the stone blocked, regimentedly empty hallway that led to their offices, their discussion focused on the future.

"What are your thoughts on next season?" Gary asked, always the contemplative one. "You still gonna coach Bobber's team?"

"I don't know. Haven't really given it much thought," Danny replied. "Why? What do you have in mind?"

Danny knew the sometimes pensive supervisor of the prison was, as anyone in charge of moving locked up men would be, cautious. "Well, what do you say about the idea of combining both of our squads?"

Danny stopped mid-hallway to listen.

"We take Bobber, Herb, Doc, Mike, and a couple others, and my best four or five," Gary began, "and we compete as one team in the same class. Juvenile I's."

"I think you may be on to something," Danny said after a moment. "I like it."

It wasn't the typical day at work for the two. As America's worst incarcerated men went about their daily routines, in the heads of the two prison supervisors preparations for a roster for the upcoming summer, still eight months away, were being made. They were thinking of twelve-to-fourteen-year-old boys as game pieces and talking about them as if they were a blooming corporation. They had the right to. These were their sons.

The list of players included Jarrod Peters, Adam "Meat" Gibbs, Bruce Luthy, and Michael Knop (Coach Gary's son), the four upper classmen, and The Brothers: Bobber, Doc, Herb, James, Mike, Zach, and a parochial kid who "wasn't too soft" named Phil Grau. It would prove to be one of the most effective combinations of athletes in the history of small-town Illinois. Not since the Macon Ironmen of 1971 would anyone see anything like it.

Six of the members were Smothers Brothers. They would bring with them to the team something that often took seasons to effect and something that sometimes never came about: a bond. Almost a brotherhood. The invisible connections that made for teamwork. There is something about baseball that, though it seems at times the most individual of team sports—players stationed on the field like a search crew—there is the secret communication, the flashing of a single index finger, a nod yes or no, the quick and deception-filled rituals of the third base coach as practiced as a priest. There's an understanding among team members and coaches, some of which can't be taught. The Smothers Brothers brought that.

Then there was Jarrod Peters and Meat. Two of the biggest meanest boys of their age in the county, with the dominance of will and personality and the bodies to back it up. Jarrod was the best pitcher in the county, at least the fiercest. He had the kind of fastball boys were scared of, even boys who loved baseball and who tried to show off. They had to talk themselves into not being afraid of it. Peters wore a perpetual scowl on his face and in the summertime shaved his head with a baseball cap on and became the hated Abbot of Baseball. If an opponent getting a hit off him infuriated him, losing a game set him into an intractable rage. Fortunately for all, he rarely lost.

If Jarrod was the backbone of the team — capable of going through an entire season without a loss — then Meat was the muscle. His great-grandfather was Bluto (it seemed), and you didn't dare cross him. He'd pick a bat out of the bag and hit a ball so hard it sounded like the ugly fruit of an osage orange splattering on an Illinois rail. Bam!

Peters and Meat — their *rule* over the narrow alley between pitcher's mound and home put the sick feeling of fear in the gut of many a kid trespassing across the chalked perimeter of the batter's box.

Every day at work, all through the fall and winter, Danny and Gary talked over the possibility. Deep inside the dark prison of Menard they chewed on the possibility. Spring would come. Spring season. That meant baseball in Chester, meant life, new life, and hope revived. You could smell hope in the new-turned soil as rich as cake and the tiny green sprouts.

But it was on a snowy night in January of that year

that the baseball season unofficially began. Knop made the short drive up to Molly's Moon. Just across the street from the high school, Molly's was the kind of small bar and greasy spoon layered with the smell of yet another chicken basket, where old men came to flirt with gum chewing waitresses, and people could get a family dinner of wings or burgers, or a union man could do some serious drinking to drown the week's frustrations. On the weekend, the bar, with its ringed metal barstools, was not unknown for arguments and fights, but on this night it was relatively quiet.

Gary walked into Molly's, nodding to some of the regulars. A row of them lined the stools in front of the televisions. There were the Johnson brothers who worked the coal mines, Mr. Miller from across the street at the school, Gritty, the local sports column editor, and then there was Butch, the owner.

"I need a Bud," said Knop loudly, nudging up to the bar.

"Everybody's your friend here," Butch joked. Just then, Gary caught a glimpse of Danny and fellow coach Fred waiting for him at one of the tables. "Your Buds are over here," yelled Freddy.

As they sat in the faint corner of the smoke-filled room, golden Budweiser cooling their throats, Merle Haggard twanging from the jukebox, they began mulling over potential line-ups.

They were well aware of the talent that was going to be on the field. However, they all knew that by combining both the older group and the younger boys certain challenges would be bound to surface. There would be challenges. "Let's face it, guys, almost all of them are in need of some kind of guidance," Freddy told the table. "I mean Jarrod and Adam are just one example."

Jarrod, Fred's son, and Meat, although lifelong friends, fought constantly, whereas, The Brothers had spent three years developing a reputation at school as both athletes—and fun lovers. Their bond was unbreakable, Smothers had long ago fallen off as too disingenuous. They were simply The Brothers.

Just a month earlier Herb, Doc, and James had received detentions for a week for splattering the playground blacktop with chewed tobacco during recess. Lucky for them it was close to the end of school or a harsher punishment may have been handed out. It was behavior such as this that came to define the boys in their latter days of middle school. Teachers began referring to them as "The Six Pack," a facile prophecy. Although the three adults knew of the potential pitfalls of a merger, none outweighed the hopes for successes. They knew good and well the baseball potential of their boys. In their experienced baseball minds, this team was going to be the team that put Chester on the baseball map. It was going to be the team that would eventually win Chester's' first ever Class "A" National Championship and potentially Chester High School's first ever State Championship. The boys were that good.

About an hour passed and the makeshift roster was set. They scribbled it down on a couple unused napkins leftover from dinner. The names and positions looked like this.

Age	Pos.	Player's Name
14	P/SS	J. Peters
14	3b	B. Luthy
14	2b/SS	M. Knop
14	C	Meat
13	P/1b/OF	Bobber
13	1b/P	Doc
13	OF	M. Niermann
13	OF	Herb
13	OF/P	P. Grau
13	C/OF	Z. Engel
13	2b	J. Knott

Danny let Knop and Peters know right away that he would be opting out of coaching with them. He was already planning on coaching Kurt, his youngest son's team. Dad's in Chester gave equal time to their sons, if they had more than one. Besides, he knew Fred and Gary along with the addition of Big Bruce Luthy, the father who rutted his own lawn with ground balls to his son, would be more than capable of handling the team.

Fred, unjokingly called "The Sheriff" by the boys, was in fact a sheriff, the lone cop in his little town of Ellis Grove. He stood six feet tall, weighed in close to three hundred pounds, had shoulders as broad as a bear's, and a head to match. He often went unshaved, and his off black fu manchu only accentuated his naturally gruff expression. Half man, half bear. It was no wonder his son Jarrod was, in his age group, the meanest kid in the county. When The Sheriff talked, people stopped in their tracks and listened. His son's fastball had something of the same effect.

Gary demanded the same respect. Warden of Menard, Gary was built like a house. His style was different than Fred's. Gary had the uncanny ability to teach and talk without yelling or using intimidation. He commanded not demanded.

Big Bruce, who had but one son, Little Bruce, loved baseball more than any dad in town. While the other dads stood cross-armed and stoically watching during a game or managed loosely from the sidelines, Big Bruce sat on the edge, living every play through his son. He would twitch his hands and bite his lip, holding back bigger emotions. You could tell if Little Bruce made an error at third simply by watching Big Bruce on the sidelines. He would pace up and down near the chalkline, like a jungle cat on an inaccessible border. But he owned the Dairy Queen in Chester, and after every victory served up ice cream to the victors like a bartender beer.

He would be the perfect guy to compliment Peters and Knop in commanding this group of young men throughout the summer of '95.

CHAPTER SIX
Meat

The first warm day of spring 1995 brought with it the scent of baseball. Leather. Dirt. A wind blowing out. Four months had gone by since that meeting at Molly's, and now the men were as excited as the boys about the summer that lay ahead of them. The first day of practice on May 19 marked the first official day of summer for the young teens. School was out, and what they waited for all year—baseball and another three months off from school—was now a beautiful reality.

As the noticeably younger members of the team, the Smothers Brothers had a slightly subdued anxiousness about them. Even though they had played with three of the older boys in junior high, Coach Peters and Coach Knop were foreign to them. The buzz, generated from the merger, was evident at the field that day. However, not everyone was beaming with joy.

The Sheriff made it evident from the start the kind of coaching style he was going to employ, an old-school, Casey-Stengel-style, no-nonsense, in-your-face, do-what-I-say coaching.

Meat was going to be the team's starting catcher. He had played for The Sheriff the previous four summers and had been friends with Jarrod since tee-ball. He and

Jarrod had bully personalities—and the size and strength to enforce their will. An ornery fourteen-year-old, Meat did his own thing with a peremptory attitude that even some teachers feared. He was big and feared nothing and took no shit from anyone. One time in Little League a kid spat too close to Meat's feet; he sprang up and pushed the kid down out of the batter's box. He brought a mentality to the team that The Brothers had never seen before and at the same time respected.

After finishing infield and outfield practice, The Sheriff split the squad into hitting groups. One group was assigned to the cages to hit off the machine, while the other was designated to face Jarrod's live pitching on the field. Meat, assigned to group two, volunteered to be the first challenger to his buddy Jarrod on the mound. Engel put on his catcher's gear. The Sheriff, taking his position behind the backstop, studied the pitches popping Engel's glove behind the plate.

The previous night's rain made it easy for Meat to dig into the batter's box. Meat knew plenty well the "stuff" that Jarrod would be throwing at him; after all he had caught him for the majority of his life. Guessing a first-pitch fastball, Meat cocked his hands back a little sooner than normal, got his front foot down, and swung as hard as he could. This overreach was not a surprise to the sly Peters. He was far from being a schmuck on the mound. After all, he had been the number one pitcher in the area for years.

He was well aware of Meat's approach to hitting. The "see it and hit it" was feckless against the heady pitcher. Peters gripped both his index and middle fingers on the left seam of the tightly wound ball, wound up, and released a gaping curveball. The free-swinging Meat swung right through it, hitting nothing but air.

Knowing the result of the first "Uncle Charlie," Jarrod knew exactly what to throw next. Another curve was in order.

The next pitch, placed better than the first, broke directly over the outside corner of the plate. There was nothing Meat could do. The black magic Easton skimmed right over the side spinning piece of cowhide.

It didn't take Peters much pondering to decide what to throw next. Peters guessed he could probably K Meat with another curveball. However, he set out to do more than just strike out his old rival: he was determined to make a point.

He placed both fingers on the ball, but instead of placing them on the left seam, he positioned them an inch apart, across the horseshoe. Engel, signaling two fingers between his crouched legs wanting the curve, Jarrod calmly shook him off. Beneath the mask, Zach grinned, slowly positioning himself on the inside corner. Raring back and firing, Peters let it go. The 80 mph fastball headed straight for the black part of the plate on the inside corner. *Pop* was the sound as it hit the catcher's mitt. Not expecting it, Meat stood frozen.

"Strike three!" yelled Sheriff from behind the backstop.

"The hell it is!" spat Meat. "Inside!" He hit the

batter's box with his bat. "That pitch was inside if I ever seen an inside pitch!"

"Get out of the box," Sheriff told him. "That ball was a strike and you know it. Next hitter!" The two went back and forth for what seemed to be five minutes.

"Freddy, if you want me out of the box, you are going to have to make me get out of the box," Meat yelled. "And I don't think you can."

The furious Sheriff made his way around the backstop, marching toward the batter's box.

The Brothers watched, frozen. They felt for the first time that they were in over their heads.

Meat stood his ground in the batter's box. He wasn't going anywhere.

As tough and stubborn as Meat thought he was, in his mind he had no doubt he could take the three-hundred-pound forty-year-old. As Freddy reached the batter's box, an eerie silence came over Cohen Field Number 2. The rest of the players crept closer to watch the action.

The Sheriff came to an imperious stop two feet in front of Meat. Just when everyone thought Meat was going to do something extremely stupid, like swinging at or pushing the much bigger and older coach, the hot-headed teen shifted gears. Whether it was fear or respect for the "old man," Meat decided to obey his old coach. Slouching back to the dugout, Meat saved face with his teammates by cussing under his breath at them.

As quick as the ordeal began, it ended. That was the start of the season. A near fight. Passion. Argument. The will to fight. The discipline not to.

The Juvenile I's went on with practice as if nothing had happened. But something had. Respect had happened.

Continuing with batting practice, the Brothers looked at each other in almost disbelief, "This is going to be an interesting season."

CHAPTER SEVEN
The State Championship:
Popeye vs. Superman

Chester's very first business was a castor oil press, established by one R. B. Servant in 1830. It may be her most enduring legacy—not counting the prison. Castor oil, the juice of the castor bean plant favored for centuries as a laxative, proved "a flourishing business until the petroleum industry made it obsolete," history reports. But, in fact, Castor Oil would live on, albeit in a form much easier to swallow. In 1894 one Elzie Crisler Segar was born in Chester, and as a young adult, he *singlehandedly revived Castor Oil in a different permutation.*

In 1919 after moving to New York to pursue his promising career in cartooning, Segar created a cartoon strip featuring an eponymous character, homage to one of Chester's earliest reasons for being: Castor Oyl, a diminutive, roly-poly, well-dressed, quick-witted adventurer. That character was joined in the strip by his sister, the century's funniest damsel in distress: Olive Oyl.

When Castor Oyl needed a tough sailor to sail his ship to Dice Island, Segar created one of the most unforgettable characters of all time. Popeye's very first line: Asked if he is a sailor, he makes this salty reply: "'Ja think I'm a cowboy?"

To this day, in honor of the Chester native who never came back home, the town annually puts on a "Popeye Picnic." Statues of Segar's characters are found at strategic, almost scavenger hunt locations about town, memorializing one of the greatest cartoons, and cartoonists, of the twentieth century. A bronze statue of Popeye stands at the Chester Welcome Center across the bridge the opposite direction from the prison.

The Old Chester Theater, where Elzie Segar once cranked the silent movies

About the same time that Segar was making it rich from

a sketch pad, another would-be cartoonist was suffering rejection. Desperate for money during the Great Depression, Jerry Siegel (from Cleveland, Ohio) sold all rights to his comic book character for $130 dollars. DC Comics still owns the rights—to Superman.

Two hours down the road from Chester is Metropolis, Illinois. Like Chester, bustling more with pickup trucks and ag business than anything else. In 1972, the Illinois House of Representatives officially acknowledged Metropolis to be the "Hometown of Superman." It was more out of entrepreneurial opportunity than pretension. A year later, the "Amazing World of Superman" museum opened in town, and Metropolis made plans to build a thousand-acre, $50 million Superman theme park. At the center of the park would stand a 200-foot-tall statue. Cars would enter driving between Superman's legs.

Thus, by such serendipity, Southern Illinois gave birth to, on the one hand, and adopted, on the other, two great characters of Americana, each known for his spectacular transfigurations. For four generations, every boy who ever brimmed with inspiration asked his mom to buy him raw spinach so he could pull it out of the can like Popeye—the likable sailor who redefined the depths of comeback.

Likewise, there's never been an American boy that went to bed at night in tight red pajamas and a cape made of a bath towel, the symbol S on his chest. Every boy needs a hero.

Every boy wants to be one.

It is more than an accident of demographics that most of the great American war heroes of the first half of the twentieth century came from farms and small towns—Sergeant York, Audie Murphy, Ernie Pyle, Dwight Eisenhower. Heroes come *from small towns where imaginations grow unbounded.*

*Popeye and Superman, heroes of unbounded imagination,
battle enemies in cityscapes and faraway lands, but their
unprovoked nature is both modest and benign. Truly, their
enemies are no different than the gnarly mouthed bully at the
Main Street Tap or a meteoric fastball you want to clobber out
of the park.*

*In the summer of 1995, two teams from the ostensible
hometowns of Popeye and Superman, respectively, would
meet in a real epic battle — on the baseball field.*

Danny and Gary's "merger" worked. The team
rolled through the first half of summer. The Juveniles
from Chester were embarrassing local teams in league
play and dismantling the competition at the regional
and district tournaments, led by the pitching of Peters
and Bobber, with run support in surplus from the
pinging bats of most everyone in the lineup.

Peters was his usual fierce self, proving his legend
by warm-up pitches that almost literally struck fear in
wide-eyed boys standing in the batter's circle. Bobber,
just turned thirteen years old, had lived and breathed
baseball for as long as he could remember. There was
nothing in the world he would rather do than play
baseball. For years, he had sat envy-eyed at sporting
events, watching Jason, his older brother, observing
how the fans reacted to big plays and flushing with
something like joy when cheers erupted. He saw how
athletes got singled out simply by making a basket or
singling to right — their names shouted and applauded
as though they were special among the town's citizens.

For stealing a base or out-foxing an opposing hitter from the mound, there seemed to be a special approval. Bobber wanted this.

He heard that throwing the ball as far as you could (the long toss), could make your arm stronger. So he would scrounge up as many baseballs as he could find in the house, walk down to the bowl (St. Mary's) and chuck long toss back and forth in the outfield grass until it was too dark to find the balls. Not only that but he learned a new grip, though he could never remember where he got it from. Later he learned it was a slider grip. He gripped the ball with his two dominant fingers, along the seams but slightly off center. He violently flung his wrist forward upon delivery, terrible for his ten-year-old arm but great for giving the pitch an animated, downward movement. No kid could touch it at either the playground or a curried ball diamond.

The Ohlau's splurged and got their three boys one of the biggest surprises of their young lives: a Nintendo. Probably it was because they got tired of the fighting and thought this magic box would calm the boys down. It didn't. It only dialed up the intensity of competition.

"Can't you do something about it?" Sharon pleaded.

Danny intervened and limited his sons to only a select few games. *Baseball Stars* was one of them. Now Bobber could play baseball all night.

By the summer of 1995, Bobber was once again pitching against boys older than himself. His record was 8–0. Peters too was 8–0, and the Juveniles as a team were undefeated in twenty games. They couldn't wait for state.

Metropolis, Illinois, home of Superman, was slated to be the host city. If Chester had Popeye, Metropolis had Superman. The tournament would be played in Metropolis City Park, two skinned out all dirt infields, a paint-chipped bench in each dugout shaded by a shoddy roof, no fence in the outfield, one foul pole down each line, a mortar block concession stand between the fields, a rusty playground for the little kids, Astro minivans and pickup trucks crunching to a stop in the gravel parking lot. A three-game series between Chester and the hometown Supermen would determine who would be champion of the entire state of Illinois.

The Supermen had a perfect record themselves, 18–0. They would prove the best competition the Juveniles had seen all summer long. They packed a powerful lineup anchored by a massively built left-handed first baseman everybody called "Big Mo." Big Mo, not only looked like a high school hitter but hit like a man. A big man.

In game one of the finals, Bobber would get the start. While warming up in the pen, he knew he had his good stuff going. His curve was breaking sharply, his fastball showing pinpoint accuracy. The seams of the ball felt familiar in his grip.

In the first, Bobber quickly went to work. He got the first two hitters to ground out on change-ups down in the zone. The third hitter, canny, worked the count to 3-2 before grounding to Luthy at third. Bruce Luthy, known by many to be the most sure-handed third baseman in all the Juvenile Class of Khoury League, bobbled the grounder and failed to make the throw.

Big Bruce, his dad, put his head down for just a moment. He'd literally hit ten thousand ground balls to that boy in their own front yard since little Bruce was old enough not to run out on the street. When his wife once complained they were killing the lawn, Big Bruce replied as the father of the great third baseman Harmon Killebrew had. "I ain't raisin' grass; I'm raisin' a son!" Big Bruce's head bobbed back up. "That's okay!" he said, smacking his fat leathery palms together. "We'll get 'em!"

Little Bruce kicked at a clod in the infield. He knew he had no excuse. The lawn of the Luthy home had prepared him for every bump in life.

That error brought Big Mo to the plate.

At the ripe age of thirteen and feeling every bit five foot six and towering, Bobber was fearless on the mound. After all, he had thrown smoke bombs through old people's windows and firecrackers at bullies. He knew Mo was a hitter to be feared. He had heard the stories of him hitting three home runs in the districts but felt no fear as the oversized 6'2", 250 pounder swaggered hungrily to the plate. Mo had been named for the great Mo Vaughn of the major leagues and held a bat like he'd held one instead of a rattle.

But there is a certain cockiness that runs through a great pitcher and Bobber, whether he came by this naturally or his older brother had pounded it into him over the years, felt that inner superiority often rise to a challenge. He liked battling Supermen. He knew, after talking it over beforehand with The Sheriff, exactly how to pitch Mo. He was going to stay away from him, not putting any pitch on the inner half of the plate. Inside pitches to Mo often ended up over the fence.

He started with a curveball, painting the outside corner for strike one. Pitch two, the slider grip, missed outside. Ball one. Pitch three, another slider, missed down and away, bringing the count to two balls and a strike. Figuring Mo would be looking fastball now, Bobber set up to throw another curve away. Only problem was, when he let go, the ball started too far left. "Oh crap," he thought. It wasn't away at all—but breaking for the inside part of the plate. Crack! Making solid contact, Mo's bat sent the ball flying into the right field sky. "It never seemed like it was going to land," Bobber said afterward. "It just kept going and going." Niermann, the Juvenile's right fielder kept running and running and running after it.

Mo had contacted the ball about as solid as anyone could hit a baseball. But in his overanxious swing, he had crushed it slightly too much on the left side, suffering it to spin sideways as it rose to the sky. It was quickly hooking toward the line. *Please go foul, please go foul, please go foul*, Bobber begged, and the umpire answered his prayer, "Foul ball!" As everyone in the park exhaled, Bobber knew he had dodged a bullet—or cannonball.

Four straight off-speed pitches. I need to stop thinking so much and challenge him with a different pitch, Bobber reasoned with himself. He caught Meat's mean glare behind the catcher's mask. Meat didn't like anyone who could hit farther than he could.

Although Bobber didn't pack a fearsome fastball like Peters, he had deceptive speed. He also had a funny way of making every pitch different, even if it was the same pitch. "Nothing ever was consistent about his pitch velocity or movement," Peters would say. He liked to watch his younger mound partner and critique him. "That's just Bobber, constantly playing with the hitters. He never held the ball the same, some pitches he would tighten his grip; with others he would loosen it. Like a cat and mouse game. Sometimes Meat would call for a curve and Bobber would deliver a fastball. Not even his own catcher always knew what was coming. He didn't want his pace of pitching to change, only his pitches. That was just Bobber being Bobber."

Instead of giving him a fastball which he would probably catch up with and hit, Bobber decided on something a little more unorthodox. *Since he was out in front of the curve, why not throw him something slower?* The logic seemed irrefutable. Bobber motioned for Meat to come to the mound. Meat was not happy about the interruption but obliged. The crowd was still unsettled from the early excitement. Mo backed off the plate and took some healthy practice swings. That last hit was just a warm-up.

Bobber, speaking into the pocket of his old glove, informed Meat in one word what the next pitch he would be throwing would be: "Eephus."

"The *eephus*?" Meat replied, incredulously. "Ok

man." Meat jogged back to the plate and crouched down in front of the umpire.

For those who do not know what an eephus is, the explanation is almost disappointing. The eephus, origin of name unknown, is a very low speed junk ball pitch. If the pitch is going to be successful, the pitcher must slow his delivery considerably to catch the hitter off guard. The only way to deal with that kind of power at the plate was to throw it off guard. Baseball is the one sport where actually trying *less* often works. In this case, the plan worked to perfection.

As Bobber slowed his windup and let go of the ball, the projectile appeared to Mo as a familiar sight headed toward the plate. Mo swung through the zone with all the grunting strength and power he could muster. But his bat flew violently past the ball. All Metropolis groaned, and the fans on the Chester side burst into in cheers and laughter. Looking on in disbelief, the city of Superman fans sat shaking their heads. Bobber had pulled that one out of his repertoire as confidently as Popeye pulled spinach out of a can.

But the battle of brawn, brains, and sheer unaccountable vicissitudes was just beginning.

The game remained scoreless until the bottom of the third inning. Metropolis walked the first man, and consecutive singles followed from the Rainman, Grau, Bobber, Peters, and Meat, five in a row resulting in four runs. Chester added an insurance run in the bottom of the fourth on singles by Luthy and Davitz, and the Juveniles secured a 5–2 victory.

The boys of Chester went lightly back to the hotel,

knowing that they would only have to win one out of two and they were Class "A" State Champs. Just one out of two.

· · · · ·

The next day brought the same late June, Southern Illinois high 90-degree heat. Arriving at the park with uniforms cleaned overnight, the kids could see the home team already out on the hot dirt and warm grass, warming up on the infield. There seemed to be a new energy.

"A team like Metropolis isn't going to go down without a fight," The Sheriff growled at the boys. "They've only f—ed up one game all season. In their minds, they are just as capable of winning this as we are."

But the advantage for Chester going into Sunday's game was obvious. They had their number one pitcher, Jarrod Peters, slated for the start. Jarrod brought with him an 8–0 record and the reason for it: a fastball that sizzled past batters like it was turbocharged. You could hear it coming in. Peters was sort of the anti-Bobber when it came to pitching. Instead of relying on finesse and precision, he went with his power.

If the first game was cat and mouse, Sunday's contest was a dogfight. Peters, effective throughout, kept Metropolis and Big Mo at bay for most of the game. The hard-headed ace of the staff did his part in securing the victory for the Juveniles. The defense behind him, however, failed to do theirs. In one inning, the sons of Chester committed four costly errors. Errors are contagious and something of the dark side of teamwork: once one brother "catches" it, the error bug, it can spread to the entire infield. The four errors contributed to five Metropolis runs crossing the plate in the fourth inning. Despite Peters' four-hit, complete game, Chester came up short, 5–4.

Now there would be a third and final do-or-die game for the championship. It would start almost immediately.

The sun seemed to redouble its own effort. The red mercury in the thermometers inched toward the top. The umpires, sweating to hydration, announced that each team would get thirty minutes to regroup and get ready for Game Three of the series.

Chester needed regrouping. After a long, hot, first game, coming within one run of securing a birth in the Class "A" Nationals, the team needed a chance to rest and regain some confidence. For the first time all summer, the Chester coaching staff was sweating over a shortage of players. Who were they going to send to the mound? Peter's was exhausted; he had pitched his heart out and watched helplessly as his own teammates booted the opportunity away. Bobber had pitched the day before and was only thirteen. But to The Sheriff, there was only one answer. Bobber again.

Craig Ohlau, "Bobber," had thrown seven innings the day before, but it didn't matter. He was the kind of pitcher who could throw twenty innings in a day, and if it hurt his arm, well then so be it. He was just the kid to put out there, stupid enough to feel no pain, chippy enough to think everyone doubted him, and competitive enough to do anything to prove them wrong. He had sat through enough Chester sporting events to know what you had to do to enliven a crowd, to be not only accepted but praised. To be a hero.

Even though the coaching staff boldly expressed their confidence in Bobber, the young pitcher sensed the over touting, heard a note of doubt. The heat was starting to beat on his forehead. His baseball cap was so soaked he could no longer use it to mop his brow. He noticed his teammates slightly turn away, turning to Gatorade and water for solace. Everyone doubted him, he thought. He felt his teammates pound him encouragingly on the back. But they doubted. The paranoia of doubt. He heard the Metropolis fans and players celebrating their momentum, trying to keep it revved up. The Chester fans, the umps, even his own team, though, he believed doubted him. A paranoia of doubt.

He would set out to prove them wrong.

• • • • •

The State Championship game saw Chester jump out to an early 2–0 lead on doubles by Bobber himself and Niermann. *That'll show 'em,* Bobber seethed through gritted teeth, as he stood up at second. After scoring, he had a few minutes in the dugout to cool off physically. But mentally he was heating up.

On the mound, Chester's young pitcher was dealing, as they say, a term that no doubt comes from poker, itself a game of skill, chance, bluff, and laying it on the line. After getting the ninth hitter to hit a weak ground ball to Knop at second, Bobber had retired the first nine batters.

But Metropolis fought back with single runs in the fourth, fifth, and sixth, while putting the clamps on the Chester offense. The top of the seventh saw Metropolis holding onto a slim 3–2 lead. "Bobber's getting tired! Bo-bber's getting ti*iii*red!" mocked the Metropolis fans. The fact that they knew his nickname both honored and angered him. Bobber, losing the precise command of each of his pitches, was obviously laboring. He loosened his cap by the bill. "Bo-bber's getting ti*iii*red! Bo-bber's getting ti*iii*red!" The fact of the matter was exactly that: he was tired. Over the last two days, he had thrown over 200 pitches from the mound and played eighteen innings of baseball in the 90-degree heat.

Both starting pitchers, in fact, were beginning to show signs of fatigue. Bobber took off his cap and tried to swipe away the pulsing heat. He nodded to his dad, The Warden, and to The Sheriff that he was all right. Meat, who seemed to be swaying behind the plate, was so soaked in sweat, it looked like it was coming through his pads. In what seemed like his last explosion of energy, Bobber fired a fastball. The Metropolis batter swung and missed. Chester ran to the dugout to get out of the sun.

Bobber's counterpart, the Metropolis ace who had battled the potent Chester lineup to near perfection most of the game, had one more daunting task to complete: shut down one of the most talented lineups in Khoury League history one last time.

The boys from Chester were up for the last inning, perhaps the last time. They knew their time was now. They hadn't come this far to let the opportunity pass. They had to dig in and push at least one run across. Silence filled the dimly shaded dugout as each player seemed to be searching inside himself to see if there was anything left after the long, hot weekend of battle. Just then, a big voice rang out from the end of the dugout.

"We aren't going to lose this game! WE ARE NOT

GOING TO LOSE!" It was Peters, at the top of his lungs.

"You're damn right we aren't!" It was Meat. The fight was back in Meat.

Screams followed as the Juvies psyched themselves up for what would turn into the most magical inning of their small town's baseball history.

Herb, first batter up, initiated it all by singling to left, Bobber followed with a double to left center, Peters lifted a home run into deep left field, Gibbs doubled down the line, Luthy singled, Niermann doubled, Knop singled, Grau singled, and Rainman walked on four pitches.

When it was all said and done, the Chester Juveniles scored eleven runs in the inning for a 13–3 victory and the title of State Champions.

They were now headed to Nationals.

Popeye—the creation of a Chester native

CHAPTER EIGHT
Wet Rats

The white foam momentarily outlined a murder scene...

Chester Community Pool

The week following the State victory was just like any other for the budding teens. The boys enjoyed their routine bike rides around town and the long hot days relaxing in the cool waters of the town's pool. The extremes of hot and cold in southern Illinois were much like the hormonal extremes of a teenage boy. In the winter, long gray drizzly February afternoons dampened everyone's spirit. Farmers could grow depressed and against that mood stirred extra cream and sugar into their coffee at the Main Street Café. Boys looked drearily out of the wet windows, their breath steaming against the cold glass, and dreamed of a green playground. But now it was the height of summer. Heat and hormones ran high.

The Chester pool was a thoughtful, modern affair, made to look like a fountain pool, with its center fountain spewing water like a smoke stack spews smoke. It was a popular gathering place for many who found nothing better to do with their summers, and these the boys referred to as "pool rats."

Pool rats were those kids for whom the lifeguards were summer babysitters. The Brothers had little respect for the "rats." Wet rats.

"What kids come to the pool every day during the summer? Don't they have anywhere else to be?" The Brothers scoffed. As baseball players, they were doing business in the heat of the day, the smothering asthmatic humidity and 100-degree temperatures. Not even the local farmers entered a field after high noon. But The Brothers had battled for two games in one afternoon to win the State Championship of Illinois. They earned their dips in the cool pool.

But what lack of respect they had for the pool regulars, the boys made up for in their love for the lifeguards. The girls, that is.

They never found themselves looking down on the lifeguards, literally down—except in that barely disguised venture up the ladder of the high dive from whose stiffly plastic flexibility a glance at the unfathomable bosom below thrilled them like the prospect of an evil bite from an Eden apple. Those girls enthroned on lifeguard stands and endued with the responsibility of saving lives were angelic. They were high school girls—developed, older, mysterious, and tanned. As one economist had quipped, likening a Wall Street algorithm to the bikini, "What it reveals is important; what it conceals is essential."

High school lifeguards needed to do nothing to earn the respect—the reverence—of the brothers but sit goddess-like on their guard chair thrones, emotionless but not unvigilant, with baby oil and sunglasses. Their eyes were hidden mysteries, their attention impossible to gain. You squinted at them with the mesmerized curiosity of an astronomer spying a new planet, of a forest ranger discovering a new tree. The fountain sprayed mist at the center of the pool the goddesses were positioned around in a way that made you feel not merely safe but guarded and happy, a Paradise, a pantheon of lifeguards, a Parthenon of possibilities. Chester community pool was a temple—with sunglassed goddesses.

Getting their attention was impossible. Unless you did something impossible.

Although each lifeguard possessed her own unique subsets of beauty, the boys were especially lured by the Goddess of goddesses who sat beneath the high dive, patrolling the deep end with her blue sunglasses and blonde waves both flashing in the sun. The boys were in awe of how the sun struck her hair, but their main focus was not heliologic. It was the shape of her legs.

"Why are you looking that way?"

"I'm just looking at her," Bobber explained. He was squinting, shading his eyes as though he were saluting Douglas MacArthur or someone, his expression frozen in the early stages of pain.

Doc saluted and squinted toward the lifeguard stand. He needed not another word of explanation.

Each trip to the pool, The Brothers tried desperately and with some creativity to impress the tanned and shapely beauty, guardian of the broach blue waters beneath the diving boards. That spot in the pool was like the bottom of a waterfall—the most coveted, but dangerous to get to. The boys tried everything to get noticed. They splashed, they feigned drowning, they made animal sounds. One time Doc made a chicken sound that really sounded like a chicken was drowning.

She rarely acknowledged that they even existed, but for a heliotropic signal from her blue shields.

Perhaps if they really almost drowned, the sudden existential question might have aroused her professional concern. She would arise, one imagined, her red swimsuit bottom so long pressed against the throne, and descend gracefully, as though it were Jacob's Ladder. But she seated there so perfectly in the afternoon heat, she was to The Brothers the shining statue of a sex symbol sporting the latest Ray-Ban sunglasses and shopping mall swimsuit. She was fat in the right places, with the kind of promising exaggeration of contour that must have lured early explorers to the West. There was something inside young Bobber than wanted to cry, "Wagon, ho!" or some such thing that he may have read in a textbook way back in a fifth grade. Every once in a while she would get up, descend (this caused a moment of breathlessness), and stride across the wet cement. That was really interesting. No glamorous babe in all of Hollywood was ever more interesting to the boys. Not even Pamela Anderson.

Although the boys were content with feasting their eyes from afar on the sun-basking beauty of Chester Community Pool, the summer was inching closer and closer to its conclusion. They needed closure on something. There was an aching need for an ending, a satisfying ending. A crowning moment. Perhaps that is what teen years are all about. The teenage years were a chapter waiting for a happy ending. Fairy tales and hero stories had planted this seed in him as a child. But now Bobber wanted the gritty reality. He wanted to be the hero, the prince. He wanted to impress Linda Sullivan. Maybe even get a kiss. Maybe he would die—nearly drown—and she would have to resuscitate our fallen hero with desperate passion. Or maybe she would bring that throne-pressed seat to the bleachers at Cohen Field, and he would hit for her the game-winning home run, and she would join the throng, and her hands would be among those holding him up, carrying him off the field, crowning him Champion of the Summer.

"Has she said a word or even made eye contact with either of us the entire summer?" Bobber said to Mike who shook his head. "We need to do something."

This seemed to be so much the opposite of hunting

on his grandpa's farm. There you waited in the brush breathlessly, hoping the quail did not spot you. Here Bobber stood *in plain view* praying for some acknowledgment.

How can we get her to notice us? Bobber thought a moment. A dangerous moment—for when a young teen boy adds thought to his passion it is like adding gasoline to a stick fire. "Do you think she would be impressed if one of us does a four off of the high dive?"

"A *four*?" Mike repeated incredulously. "I sure as heck ain't gonna do a four! I can't even hardly do one." He turned to Bobber. "How many can you do?"

"Well, I can do two off the low dive," Bobber gulped, "what if I tuck and do as many flips as I can, not worrying about how I land?" He squinted up at the diving board. It was high as a basketball rim. He had spent many an hour dreaming of dunking at ten foot, but now his ambition was to launch from that very apex. "It can't hurt too bad if I'm tucked, right?" he reasoned scientifically. "She'll have to notice then."

Doc padded over and joined the consultation. Without his Elton John's he could only squint with a scrunched nose. "Whatta ya lookin' at?"

"Bobber's gonna try a four."

"What the hell!" Doc often got 100s in Math, and the quick calculation he seemed to have done in his head gave no confidence to his Brother. But Love is incalculably greater even than Math as stupidity has it all over Wisdom.

Although the plan seemed absurd, the boys had

done things more foolish before. There was, for example, the ill-conceived butt crack incident. But in all of their time at the Chester pool, five years of childhood, the boys had never seen a four accomplished off the high dive by anyone. No one ever did *four* flips.

"Dude, no one can do four," Mike said, slapping Bobber on the bare back. "Land this and you'll be a legend."

Bobber, with some rising reluctance, decided to go for it. After all, you only live once—unless you're a Buddhist, he had heard. He was no Buddhist. He took each of the ten cold steel steps slowly as he made his way to the temporary safety of the high dive platform. The diving board was approximately ten feet above the water, and if one were to catapult correctly, and with enough passion, one could propel a bodily projectile fifteen feet into the air at apex. The four flips would then be—mathematically impossible.

But calculations were, like all plans aforethought, less valuable than the actual final score.

As Bobber slowly crept toward the end of the board, feeling the roughness beneath his feet, he willfully released his grip on reality. He glanced down at his buddies saluting him below and then back to the beautiful lifeguard. Mike padded over to the other side of the pool to get a better angle on the noble tragedy that what was about to occur.

The Goddess, realizing something odd was about to go down on her watch, noticed the skinny, buzz-cut seventh grader standing in the middle of the board.

Bobber looking straight into the lifeguard's mirrored glasses and with something like a drug in his veins lipped, "This is for you," and with that, trotted to the end of the board, leaped as high as his skinny legs could take him, and on the strength of the spring propelled himself into the sunshine. One flip—two—three fli—!

A small crowd had gathered poolside. All eyes looked to where the white foam momentarily outlined a murder scene. A long moment later, Bobber emerged from under the water, slightly embarrassed and in much discomfort. Through a grimace of pain, he mustered what looked to be a smile. He lay on his back, floating on top of the water, feeling an unnatural needling and tingle throughout his entire body. His sinuses stung with chlorine. Feeling like a thing about to go either up to heaven or down a drain, he peered up at the throne.

She is going to do something, he thought to himself. *She has to*. His body and face bespoke forlorn, helpless, needy, *wanting*.

Slowly lifting her glasses, the Goddess looked down at the skinny thirteen-year-old rotating on the surface. And smiled.

The only thing Bobber knew to do was to smile back.

It was worth it, all the pain. A lesson for life. Mike hunched over the side of the pool and helped his Brother out. Doc and Herb scampered over, their bare feet slapping the concrete deck. They helped their brother out.

"Dude, that was awesome! I can't believe you did that," they congratulated their Brother, admiring the red and purple welts on Bobber's back like modern art critics. They decided together their day at the pool was over. Their summer was almost made. Just one more thing.

Tomorrow was Nationals.

CHAPTER NINE
Big Mo and the Quarter Push

It's déjà vu all over again
–Yogi Berra

Yogi Bera was right. The Juveniles would be making a return trip to the town where just a week before they had burst forth like a summer storm in the final inning. It just so happened that Metropolis had put in to host the Class "A" National tournament. Chester's first-round game would be against a team from the baseball crazy town of Reidland, Kentucky.

So The Sheriff loaded up his Juveniles in a small caravan of minivans, and the champions of the Illinois Class "A" Khoury League headed south again: The Brothers Bobber, Doc, Herb, Rainman, Mike, and Zach and Phil Grau, plus Meat and Peters and Knop and Luthy.

The trip back to the roaring city of Metropolis was made not so much with the swagger of conquerors as with the goofiness of small-town boys who were getting to stay at a hotel again, something some of them had only experienced for the first time the previous week. The little free soap samples (those could come in handy on Halloween) and the tightly tucked sheets and the air conditioner you could turn to 60 below zero, it seemed, had been novelties during the three-game, one-night affair with the Metropolis team. Now these amenities seemed positively boring.

Boys who do not always know how to behave in a small town will certainly exploit their inability in a "big city" like Metropolis, especially under the pressure of the constant sense of exploration that has led Mississippi River town boys for decades to go too deep into caves, too deep into waters, and too deep into video stores.

The caravan came rolling into Metropolis filled with clowns. Young teens do not concern themselves with future eventualities, such as the most important baseball game of their lives the next day, as much as older teens do. The idea of "mental preparation" is no good for a boy who can't even remember to pack his socks. There was only sense of fun and adventure, and when The Sheriff opened the door of the Astro minivan he was driving, out came Bobber and Doc laughing, their faces striped from a Licorice Whip fight.

It was at the BP gas station next door to the Hotel 6 that the boys found a diversion in the "Quarter Push" machine. Now all that is said of a thirteen-year-old's inability to plan ahead must be qualified. But here by "mental preparation," little connotation of intelligence was to be attached to the word "mental." The boys huddled together outside the gas station. They now knew what the night would bring.

The BP possessed a couple of quarter push machines whose carelessly accumulated quarters looked to the boys like the cherries on a Las Vegas one arm bandit sparkling in the eyes of opportunity-minded adults. These machines, which have since been made illegal for gas stations to manage, let alone for thirteen and fourteen-year-olds to play, are filled with quarters that encourage the risking of quarters to push the money in the machine over the edge into a pit where the lucky player can then collect them.

"Maybe we'll strike it rich!" said Mike. The conclusion was just beyond self-evident. But the boys were feeling lucky.

It wasn't until after lights were out that the seven would even have a chance at getting out of the prison walls of the hotel room without a parent noticing. Four of the dads there, including Bobber's, in fact, worked at a prison. The Sheriff was, it could be taken for granted, an actual sheriff. But at 10:05 p.m., the Brother's hotel room phone rang.

"You guys ready?" It was Peters.

Raj, the hotel clerk, by now knew the boys. He had gotten to know them the week before. He watched with unjudging eyes as the boys, as inconspicuously as an entire team breaking curfew can, slipped past the front desk. "It is 11 o'clock. Shouldn't you guys be in bed? You got a big game tomorrow."

Teenage boys on a mission are respectfully impervious to the advice of an adult, which sounds remarkably like the call of the challenge itself that is luring them out to take it on. "You watch out for his curveball," is not a reason for a thirteen-year-old to cower back in the dugout anymore than "You watch out for her curves" could keep boys from the town swimming pool. No reason nor morality nor reverse psychology can redirect a misguided youth headed toward a purpose. He is more missile than missionary. Perhaps sensing this, Raj said simply in deep Calcuttan English, "Be gareful."

At the back of the BP gas station and quick stop shop stood the Quarter Push Machine on four sturdy legs, like the old pinball machines that had seduced the teen boys of the previous generation. Dozens of silver disks, quarters, abutted and lay atop each other beneath the glass, as though a rich poker player had grown tired of counting his winnings, left for the night, and the piles had fallen over on top of each other. Lying slippery on top of the quarters, carelessly left behind and folded to show the 5 and the 10, were two bills.

"That's ten bucks!" Rainman said, as though none of them had seen a ten dollar bill before. The barrier of glass seemed like a moral boundary. They were almost thankful for it. Had those bills been spotted in a gutter on Main Street, the find would have been incredible, but the element of unattainability, which had made ventures to the swimming pool so irresistible, added worth to the dollar.

The ultimate row of quarters beneath the glass lay precariously close to the cliff, some overhanging so that it was easy to imagine an avalanche of quarters spilling into what would be your coffer.

The boys studied the collection of quarters beneath the glass as a team of microbiologists might observe cellular division. There were fingerprints on the glass as interesting to the keen-eyed boy as the quarters, as though some den of bears had tried to paw through the plate glass of the Cupcake Pantry back in Chester.

"Someone's been here!" Doc keenly observed, suggesting the urgency of their mission.

"Them's our fingerprints," Peters scowled. He was the oldest of the group, the veteran of the team and his voice commanded respect like his fastball, just from the sound of it.

The boys, eight of them to be exact (one of the parochial school kids had opted to stay in bed, that being his Catholic prerogative) each came with a small collection of quarters in his own pockets. Had Raj at the hotel not abrogated responsibility by returning to the seemingly pressing duties of a late-night desk clerk, he might have heard the small, muffled jingles as the boys stole out. It had taken an hour for the boys to gather enough quarters for true investment. Most of their quarters had been procured from the Bill Change machine in the little hotel laundry room, others by standing on their heads in the family minivan to check between seat cushions. As inconspicuously as the entire infield (minus one) and outfield and starting rotation of a teenage baseball team can, they walked into BP and made their way to the back where the boxes of Coca-Cola and Orange Crush were stacked in a soda pop wall.

"We split it according to how old you are," Peters told the boys.

"No way!" Bobber objected. "You're the oldest!"

Peters smiled slyly. He'd been caught. "Aw right, we split it even." The "it," of course, was the treasure chest of silver coins that would soon be theirs by all probabilities. After all, they had their ammunition; now all they had to do was load the machine.

"I'll go first," said Peters, and Meat butted in line behind him. There was no getting Meat out of line. Only The Sheriff, who was snoring loudly back in Room 111, had ever done that.

Peters rolled in a quarter as the boys stood with trembling excited paws on the glass as though to bless it, the naked quarters only inches below. One of the legs of the Quarter Push was actually *chained* to the wall. That would appear to dismiss one of the ideas that Meat had proposed, the machine being so close to the back door that led into an alley.

Peters quarter rolled stickily into the slot, reappeared beneath the glass, and nudged the other quarters. They barely moved.

"We got this," said Bobber, always confident, in spite of the evidence. "Faith is the evidence of things not seen," his mother quoted the Bible, and they had not seen a thing, not yet.

"My turn!" said Meat, and not even Peters disallowed it. Meat's quarter was pushed in with a fat and powerful thumb. It made no difference. It joined fecklessly the collection of quarters that seemed magnetically to be arranging themselves into a molecule of silver.

Then Bobber took his turn. The boys actually wanted Bobber to go. He had some kind of thing about him that caused luck to happen. Sometimes the luck was bad luck, such as the time the blue bomb bounced into the Taylor's window, but sometimes it was good, as when his slider was hitting the groove, and no batter in twenty-five miles of Chester could touch it.

Bobber pinched his lips and studied the quarters. He could feel the gear-like ridges of the quarter in his thumbs as he felt the seams of a baseball. As the part of the Quarter Push machine that moved back and forth and swept the new quarters into the pile reached just the right position, Bobber plucked his quarter in. It landed flat, was pushed by the life-like mechanisms of the machine toward the others and ever so frustratingly nudged the collection within a fraction of the edge.

The boys considered this great progress and Bobber received a few thankful pats on the back. In turn, Doc, Herb, Rainman, Mike, and Zach tried their luck, and when Rainman's quarter nudged three others over the edge, it seemed like a reenactment of Rainman's triple down the left field line against Macon earlier in the summer. From the boys came the kind of reaction that was making addicts of an entire generation of gamers, from little nerdy boys who couldn't swing so much as a 32 ounce bat to man-size boys such as Meat who liked to pick up a whole bag of bats and swing them around in the batters circle just to show off his strength.

Peter's took possession of the three quarters that Rainman's drop had won for the team, and the boys watched with near reverence and hope as quarter after quarter dropped into the machine making widow's mite contributions if not actually causing the concatenation they wished for.

The boys end up losing $25 dollars to the Quarter Push machine, their pockets empty. Their mouths were tired of awing, as they stared through the glass. More coffin than coffer.

Then Meat got the ingenious idea of picking up the machine. "Stand back," he ordered. It was the same strength he had used the winter before to pick up that boulder to throw in the back of Bobby Lanham's pickup truck as a ballast, so the boys could go rampaging out on the snow-covered country roads. You don't get a good snow in southern Illinois that often and you better take advantage of it—even if you have to borrow your dad's pickup truck and you don't have a license.

Meat pushed everyone out of the way and picked up the Quarter Push Machine by himself, and just as the thrilling spill of cascading quarters sounded, so did an alarm. There is a reason all Quarter Push Machines are fitted with no tilt alarms and would later be made illegal in Illinois.

The boys hightailed it out the back where no getaway car was waiting. A minute later, without saying goodnight to Raj, they dive between the tight-fitted sheets of their hotel beds.

Raj was right. They did have a big game tomorrow.

~~~

They'd never played a team from that far south before. These Kentucky boys would have deeper drawls and, it was suspected in advance, suspect birth certificates. In the Little League World Series there was always the suspicion that the boy from the Dominican Republic or somewhere threw like he was sixteen years old — because he actually was.

But Reidland, Kentucky, proved no match for the Chester boys. The first inning saw the Chester Juveniles score eight runs on four errors. In the next game, the Supermen from Metropolis also made quick work of their out of town foe, setting up a classic rematch of the State Tournament finals a week before. Chester's record was now 23–1, Metropolis's was 20–2, the teams' only losses coming against each other the weekend before.

In Game 3 of the double-elimination tourney, against the Supermen, Jarrod Peters did what he did best. He hurled yet another masterful game, allowing Chester to roll to a comfortable 10-4 win and putting them one game away from the much-dreamed-of "National Title."

The boys headed back to the hotel, excited at what lay in front of them. They were fully aware of what was at stake tomorrow. There would now be no more striding past Raj. This time, they would have to *sneak*.

Ever since George Khoury had founded the league in 1934, at the depth of the Great Depression when farmers whose crops failed in the field turned to baseball for fun, no team from the small river town the boys called home had ever brought home a Class "A" title. They knew what an accomplishment like this might mean to the town. It was a town that honored her sons. A town that erected statues even to fictional heroes. A town whose fathers waited expectantly for them to do what they had been told they could do.

After being banished to their rooms for the Quarter Push fiasco from the night before (Raj's cousin owned BP), the boys felt a little cramped. They needed something to pass the time. Neither sleep nor TV seemed alluring. They needed some good, clean fun.

Lying on their two hotel beds, four of The Brothers were brainstorming for ideas—when the phone rang. Was it Pete scheming up another plan? It was Danny Ohlau, Bobber's dad, making sure his boy and The Brothers were securely in their rooms. It was 10:15 p.m. Breakfast was scheduled for 7 a.m. for the Ohlau's. Disappointment dissolved to comfort. There is something comforting about hearing your dad on the other end of the line, even an annoying phone call that de-privileges and frustrates your whole plan for an evening. Not every kid got that call. And only by their unspoken envy did Bobber realize that he had it good. His dad was checking on him.

Danny Ohlau never spoke a word at home of his job in the prison, nor ever spoke a word to the prisoners of his family. "Nobody in there needs to know a thing about your family," he would say after retirement. He didn't even have a family picture on the wall of his fairly bare office in the prison. There was no connection between the one and the other. But when you have three sons, your job as father and warden are strangely similar at times. "Don't you boys go sneaking out," he quietly told Bobber.

Then he made sure to relay this message to his son from Bobber's mom: Sharon planned on the whole family attending church before the game. It didn't matter that it would be church in enemy territory, Metropolis. Twenty years of marriage and three sons had not taken the fear of God from her—but only made it more vital. Church started at 9:00 am, while the game was scheduled for noon, leaving the family ample time to praise the Lord and imbibe the sacraments, then get to the park. "Spending at least an hour each week with God in prayer or church is the least a person can do for him- or herself," Sharon would say. "Peace and blessings come to those who keep God in their lives."

It was funny how perfectly opposite church and prison were, Bobber felt, at times the one feeling like the other but the other (or so he imagined) never feeling like the one. Bobber slipped himself between the hotel sheets like a letter into an envelope. Then he closed his eyes to pray.

Then he heard in the darkness a voice: "Tomorrow there is only one thing left for us to do." It was Doc, who occupied the other side of the bed. The line was from a movie that The Brothers had watched more than once together. Bobber in the dark, with the lights from BP spraying diffusely through the crack in the curtain, waited for the line.

"Win the whole freaking thing."

.   .   .   .   .

As the morning sun now diffused through the hotel curtains, the day the boys had dreamed of all their young lives was upon them. Each family did their own thing that morning. Some worshipped, others slept in, while a few made their way out to a bigger breakfast than the little hand-cranked Fruit Loops and stale, dilute orange juice the hotel offered. At 10:30, the team gathered at the park for batting practice. After the pre-game rituals were taken care of, the coaches huddled up to talk.

The main point of conversation was who was going to start. Pitching Luthy the first game against Reidland the day before was a big luxury for the Juveniles—all those games of catch with his dad in the front yard had paid off. Bobber was now fresh. The Sheriff, The Warden, and Big Bruce all nodded to each other. "Bobber," they agreed and tossed him the ball. "Go win us a national championship," The Warden said, as if he were just sending him to the corner store for bread. If the team struggled and lost, Doc or maybe even Jarrod could then take the ball in Game Two. Dads had something that boys didn't always have: foresight, a sense of consequences.

The home plate umpire signaled the beginning of the game. "Play ball!" he growled fatly, and the National Championship game was underway.

Chester took a 4–0 lead into the top of the third, as Bobber continued to hold off the Supermen in the 90-plus degree Sunday afternoon heat. But Metropolis would not quit. They scored two runs, and Chester led 4–2 going into the final inning. The two and three hitters from Metropolis got back-to-back singles sparking a potential two-out rally in the seventh and final inning. Bobber first tried to blame church. But one glance up at the sun bowed his head. It wasn't the strength of the Lord that was failing him; it was *his own* strength. He heard a voice from the stands that he only rarely heard during a game. It was soft-spoken and deferential. It was his mom's. "You can do it, Jason."

The Metropolis fans on one side and the Chester fans on the other came to the fences and clawed the chain link.

Strutting to the plate to hero-welcoming cheers from Metropolis and taunts from Chester, was "Big Mo," more indomitable than ever. No one clapped harder for him than the runners on first and second. He stood for the winning run with one out left in the game.

"Big Mo" had already doubled and singled in the game off of the Chester lefty whose pitch count was now well into the triple digits. At the plate spitting into his huge hands was perhaps the most dangerous batter in Khoury League history.

Blocking out of memory the prior successes of the Metropolis cleanup man, Bobber set his mind to one thing. This at bat and this at bat alone would determine the outcome of the game. "Time out," Meat said to the ump as he removed his mask and began slowly walking to the mound with a patience and a stride as indomitable as Mo's. There was something comforting about the meanness of Meat when he was on your side. The man who could lift a Quarter Push machine the way Chief in *One Flew Over the Cuckoo's Nest* pulled the sink off the wall would let no obstacle—not even chance—stand in his way.

Meat reached the mound. "How we gonna pitch him here?" he wanted to know.

"Let's go after him, and if he hits it out he hits it out," Bobber shrugged.

"Sounds good to me," Meat smirked and slid his mask back down over his face as grimy as a 5 o' clock coal miner's.

Crouching back behind the plate, Meat signaled for the fastball with one finger between his shin guards. Nodding yes, Bobber delivered. The pitch, sailing high for ball one sent the Superman fans into a frenzy. Chants began ringing out from the Metropolis faithful. "Bob-ber's get-ting ti*ii*red! Bob-ber's get-ting ti*ii*red!"

"Oh-lau! Oh-lau!" responded the Chester faithful, including one churchgoer who rarely lifted her voice but in praise to the Lord.

Bobber knew the personal note from Metropolis was to be taken not so much an offense but as a sign of respect. They knew his name.

Chester knew it too. "Oh-*lau*! Oh-*lau*!" It sounded like the chant of a bullfight.

Bobber twisted the ball in his hand like he was

opening a can and glanced unworriedly at the two base runners. He wasn't about to give way to any concerns. Meat gave the same signal. *He's getting tired*, Bobber could tell; Meat couldn't think of another pitch. Bobber agreed with Meat's finger. But again the fastball sailed high, and the chants now became song:

"Bobber's get-ting ti*i*red! Bob-ber's get-ting ti*i*red!"

Never stop thinking, he remembered his dad telling him once. *But don't overthink.* The immediacy of the moment was like that of a man dying of thirst in the desert—with a wellspring lying just ahead. You just had to keep clawing, keep believing. Not give in. Never give up.

Figuring Mo, now having the advantage 2–0 in the count, would be looking for another get-me-over, Bobber decided on spinning up a curveball. Meat could barely remember to put a second finger down. Bobber nodded when he finally did.

"He reached into his empty bag of tricks and pulled out some good pitches at the end of that game," his dad observed after the game. His dad knew the arm, the grip, the competitiveness of the boy. It was his son.

The curve broke sharply across the inside corner for strike one. But the pitch didn't silence the chants. They crescendoed both for and against him as he toed the rubber.

What should I throw next? Bobber mused in his head. He had only one advantage over Mo, and that was Foreknowledge. *Why not another curve?*

Another sinking curve on the corner froze Mo for

strike two. Mo had yet to swing his lumberous slumberous bat. And that was exactly what Bobber wanted — nothing out of Mo.

Under the bill of his cap, Bobber glanced furtively at Mo. Mo was mad. Furious. Mo digging into the batter's box looked like a bull snorting to get out of a pen.

An eephus pitch was not going to work this time. Bobber knew what he needed to do. He had one advantage over Mo, one final advantage, and he was about to use it. Use it up. He shook off two signals from Meat, who was beginning to teeter from exhaustion behind the plate. Mo waited, his bat held high like he was about to club a bobcat, his nostrils gaping.

Bobber took a deep breath of the hot dusty air and gripped the ball tightly across the seams. Raring back, he let go the pitch that no one was expecting him to throw — a four-seam fastball that pierced the inner half of home plate. Mo stared in impotent disbelief as the pitch crossed the black part of the plate and popped into Meat's glove. "Stee-rike three!" sang the umpire with the last of his saliva.

One heaping, joyful, and injurious dog pile, melted ice water baths for the coaches, hugs and high fives later — the Chester boys were National Champions.

Front Row L-R: Zach, Bobber, Herb, Phil Grau, Rainman, Doc, Mike
Knop
Back Row L-R: Norm Grau, The Sheriff, Jared Hasemeyer, Jack
Cowan, Jarrod Peters, Big Bruce Luthy, Little Bruce Luthy, T'Bone
Hasemeyer, Mike Niermann, Meat, Dan Ohlau, The Warden

CHAPTER TEN
The Last Funny Bomb Threat
in America

Baseball is perhaps the only game where one man works against another where the ball, as soon as it leaves the one man, becomes a symbol. That is why baseballs are auctioned off after a great accomplishment and set in trophy cases. They are signed—and this increases the value by explicitly reestablishing the relationship to the man. In 2005, a priceless vellum scrap of the Holy Bible sold on the internet for $35,000 dollars. The same week, one of Mark McGuire's home run balls sold for $75,000. Which leads one to ask: If a manuscript of the Holy Bible flew over the left field wall at Wrigley Field, would two fans even fight over it? It is no slight to religion to claim that baseball is the first game in America to produce idols.

Late night sleepovers are not occasions for sound thinking any more than they are for sleeping. These are especially insomniac in the wake of a national championship. They are for the late night, hell-bent, end times, take-a-chance, sleeplessness-induced machinations that will either entertain or haunt you the rest of your life.

There was, in fact, a notable absence of genius in The Brother's post-victory plans, yet the sheer stupidity of it is the same that has inspired generations of boys to do the same. An action without thought. An action without consequences—until morning dawns. There's a reason the sun comes gradually, for otherwise men would all be caught out on the street at one time or another in our skivvies.

Since the conclusion of "the summer to remember," life went normally on for the juveniles. If it wasn't one thing, it was another. The Smothers Brothers were getting in more trouble now than at any other time in their young lives. Being in eighth grade was showing. The haughty boys now believed they were in control of the school. Oh, how they were wrong.

The start of school began rocky for The Brothers. Mr. Lochead seemed particularly uptight. He seemed to get mad at the boys for things as innocent as smashing bottles into the recycling bin too aggressively. The principal's office became somewhat of a second home to them. It didn't help that The Brothers would sometimes refer to him as "Lockhead," in hearing distance. The Principal seemed determined to set the boys right. Each and every time the boys made the trip down the long, carpeted hallway to his office, he had a moral or inspirational story to tell. He would squeeze the knot on his tie and relate again the time he played basketball for a small college in Indiana, how he was one of the smallest guys to tryout and still made the team, or how he worked his way through grad school getting to where he was today, or describing to the respectfully listening Brothers the commitments one had to make to be successful, as he was. No matter what it was, the boys would listen. That is, up until he started to mention *behavior*.

"Boys, I like you guys—as a matter of fact, I would want my sons to grow up like you. But I don't want them to treat people the way you do." Here the boys would tolerably lower their heads or shift their eyes or look out the window toward the playground. "You shouldn't say or do hurtful things to others, especially your friends. If you do, you will no longer have those friends." Mr. Lochead searched for more to say but then simply decided on a version of The Golden Rule that should suffice: "For gosh sakes, just be good to one another."

The Smothers Brothers were anything but good to each other. When they weren't wrestling around trying to get "The Title" (the equally innovative name for the championship belt with oversized buckle that the group passed around to the latest member who won a particular wrestling match), they would be pestering each other about their looks, the girls each was talking to, the lack of girls each was talking to, how strong each of them was, their arm size, penis size, haircut, you name it, they would be harassing each other about it. Perhaps the young principal was right. The Brothers needed to grow up and be more mindful young men. But maturity comes only in time not in teaching. This group of small-town eighth graders had a mind of their own.

Nonetheless, the boys *were* growing up. In their minds they were all wise beyond their years. In Chester like many other small towns in America, a young man's freedom is cherished more than anything else in the world. The freedoms that were allowed to be experienced shaped these young men more than one would know. And Chester offered freedom, once the school bell rang, that is. For one thing, it was a safe town. There was not a dark alley let alone a front yard that any boy was afraid to walk. In fact, if you were a boy in Chester, you were more *feared* than afraid. The memory of the blue smoke bomb hovered over Bobber not like a cloud but a mantle.

It wasn't until around this time, eighth grade, though that the boys really started to come into their own when it came to individualized and experimental thinking. Instead of the hometown Farm Fresh milk being their drink of choice, other refreshments, such as the ones not suitable by law for young people, started to dissolve their thirsts. And other thirsts were rising too...

. . . . .

"Damn my legs are tired," Mike announced after warmups. It was Friday night in the middle of November. Grade school hoops season was in full swing.

"Dude, my legs are shot too," replied Herb trying to stretch out his calves. "Me too," said Doc. "What about yours, Bobber?" asked Mike. "Mine feel like jello," Bobber answered.

"Maybe it wasn't such a good idea of wearing ankle weights all day," Doc suggested. "It was Coach Kordys' idea."

"At least our socks look good," Herb chimed in. "We can't lose with these. These are Nike's." Herb pulled stretched the victory logo up to his calves.

The boys had hopes of beating their arch rival, the Murphysboro Red Devils that evening. The Devils featured an eighth grader by the name of Broadnax who could do something that had perhaps never been seen before in small-town Illinois junior high basketball: he could dunk. After a couple of dunks by the 6'3" Broadnax and a last-second buzzer beater coming up short for the Chester Jackets, the Brothers gathered in the tiny locker room of their grade school known as "The Dungeon."

"So what's going on tonight?" Doc asked the rest of the group. "You guys want to have a sleepover?"
"Where at?" the group replied.

"I vote Mike's," said Bobber.

"I vote Bobber's," said Herb.

Scoffing, Mike replied, "Danny won't let us stay over at Bobber's. We lost tonight."

"You know how he is when we lose" Bobber acknowledged tying his high tops. He knew he'd be walking home.

"Well, Mike's it is," Doc confirmed. "Anyways, your mom makes the best pancakes."

Thus, another classic sleepover was agreed upon. This time however, Mike had an idea to add a little spice to the party.

With The Brothers all gathered in the Niermann basement, a popular sleepover spot, Mike declared he had a "surprise" for the group tonight. "What is it?" asked Doc. "Are we gonna watch *The Carpenter* again?" referring to the XXX-rated movie Joe kept in his workbench.

"No it's not *The Carpenter*," Mike told them. "But it will take our minds off of the game, and it will definitely be better than banging nails all day." The group hawed — in private remembrance of the theme of *The Carpenter*.

Just then, Mike went over to the telephone. The Niermann's still had, like most people in Chester, a long-corded land line. The boys overheard a voice coming from the adjacent room. It was Mike on the phone.

"Hey. What are you guys up to...? Do you think maybe you could do us a favor tonight?...Bobber, Doc, Herb, and James are all over here, and we were kind of wondering if you could bring us something... Ok sounds good. Bye." Mike returned to The Brothers. "It will be here in twenty minutes."

After around twenty minutes of sitting on the couch watching Michael Jordan and the Chicago Bulls toy with Shawn Kemp and the Seattle Supersonics, through the fuzz of the pirated signal from WGN-TV out of Chicago,

Mike led the crew on a walk up Riverview Boulevard, the street adjacent to the Niermann home. It was a nice night, Indian summer in southern Illinois, and the pleasant street lights exposed only the beautiful parts of the town and guided the boys like stars guide sailors. The drying leaves of the elm trees clicked together in the branches like calloused snapping fingers. There was rhythm and beauty in the nights. While hiking up the Boulevard, The Brothers noticed what looked to be an old red Dodge Dakota, brake lights shining, stopped on the side of the road at the top of the hill. As the boys made their way in the direction of the truck, the truck slowly pulled away as the Brothers approached the spot where it was parked.

"Hey," said Doc, as though a mystery had just eluded them.

But beside the road, next to a tree, visible in the bowed streetlight light, sat a brown grocery bag. It was filled with two six packs of cold Michelob bottles. Not even Budweiser—which was made in St. Louis, whose symbol was so associated with the St. Louis Cardinals. Michelob was made by Anheuser-Busch too, but it was a rich man's beer, a beer, as the advertisements said, "for connoisseurs."

"*Oui, oui,*" said Doc as he ogled at the prize.

"Dude, who was that in the truck?" Bobber wanted to know.

"You'll never guess, and I can't tell you," replied Mike, smirking with the kind of advantage any boy wants to have over the rest of his peers.

"Niermann shut the hell up," Herb smirked back. "We know who it was."

Taking the brown bag to the back patio behind the house, The Brothers sat choking down the suds. Surprisingly, some of The Brothers had already acquired a taste for the brew. It only took an hour for the twelve pack to disappear.

"Who wants the last three? I get one," said Mike.

"I'll take one," replied Doc, Herb, and James.

The time was getting late. The clock said midnight but, refueled, the boys had some energy left in them. Instead of going to bed, Mike presented an insane idea.

"Let's call my neighbor Jim and tell him there is a bomb in his house."

Now it must be said in some defense of the indefensible that those were the days before 9/11 was even imaginable and the horror of the Timothy McVeigh bombing in Oklahoma City the previous April had somehow not resonated with the boys. Their unshakeable concept of "bomb" was the kind that had flushed the Taylor's from their old house or the little ten cent popper whose ignition string you tied to your dad's car window, so that when he got in at night and cranked it up, it popped and he'd come and jump on you in bed to tell you how you had almost scared him.

The boys had tried bomb scares before. Earlier in the summer Bobber, Mike, Doc, and Doc's brother Greg (known only as G) were messing around in Bobber's room, whose bedroom window looked out on the Spinach Can Collectibles shop, a Popeye-themed store next door. There is still argument over who is to be credited with the idea, but the short of it is that they decided to call the Collectibles and make them come out the back door, which was facing the window of Bobber's room and the roof of the Ohlau's house where The Brothers used to sit out and watch the trucks go by. They came up with the one idea they thought would work, a bomb threat. Mike had the best voice and was nominated for the honor.

"There is a bomb in your store!" Mike alerted them. "The only way you can get out alive is exit out the back—if you go out the front, the bomb will go off. Have a nice day," Mike ended politely.

It didn't work. No one came out.

It was these kinds of crazy and ill-conceived ideas that the brothers were notorious for. What might have only seemed clever on Budweiser seemed pure genius on Michelob. Emboldened and bleary from beer, The Brothers dialed Jim.

Jim, mid-40s, a Boy Scout leader, thick round glasses, half gray bowl-cut hair, worked some place with a dress shirt and tie. That seemed sort of funny to the boys.

In a sleepy voice, Jim answered, "'ullo."

Mike let him have it. "Sir, there is a bomb in your house. Come out the front door or your house is going up in flames."

"What? A *bum*?" replied the confused old man.

"A bomb, sir. And the only way it will not detonate is for you to exit out of the front door immediately. So get out of your house! Now! Have a nice night, sir."

After a brief pause, they heard a click. Laughing hysterically, The Brothers couldn't believe what they were witnessing. The old man either knew it was Mike, didn't believe it was true, or he didn't care if he died in a fiery inferno. He hung up the phone and left it off the hook.

"Dang, now what?" The boys thought aloud.

The adventurous eighth graders didn't feel that they were ready to sleep their Friday night away just yet. There was one more idea left in the creative minds of the idiot youths. The brains behind the next plan were the only non-intoxicated ones of the group, Bobber's and Doc's. Their plan required the use of Mike's walkie-talkie set that was stashed away upstairs in his closet.

"Hopefully mom is sleeping," Mike said. "If not, there is no way I'm getting them." There was only one person Mike really feared, and that was his mother.

Making his way through the upstairs kitchen, Mike experienced an eerie silence in his own home. He had never crept around in it before. The boys heard the door to Mike's room open as he entered. "Good, he made it," they whispered, waiting breathlessly in the basement. When Mike's footsteps began to again cause the old wood floor beneath him to creak, they figured he was in the clear. Suddenly stopping, the footsteps ceased as a woman's voice interrupted the silence. It was Linda Niermann, his mom.

A wonderful lady, Linda was a wonderful wife and proud mother of two boys, Mike and Ed. She loved her boys more than anything. Ed would grow up, become a marine, play some college football, and got a job as a teacher, while Mike too would play college football and become a salesman in the banking industry. Perhaps his first trial in the art of sales came at this very moment. Confronting him in her pajamas, his mom asked, "What in the name are you doing? It's one o'clock."

"I'm taking the walkie-talkies downstairs, Mom. We're gonna play a little game of hide and seek. We're going to bed in a little bit. I promise."

It was freeing to the conscience of all The Brothers that Mike had not lied. After all, they were counting on pancakes in the morning.

The footsteps once again began clacking through the upstairs kitchen. The basement door opened as Mike began descending down the old linoleum-covered stairs. "We're good," he said with a grin.

Now that they had the walkies, Doc had something to say. He had the master plan all thought out. "We're gonna sneak out, take the walkies over to Brian's." This was a neighbor two houses down, whom the boys thought would be a more gullible participant in their late-night prank. He didn't go to work in a shirt and tie and had the cover of trees in his yard. "Put one walkie on his doorstep," Doc carefully instructed, "knock on his door, and when he answers, we'll give him shit through the walkie." West Point could not have come up with more ingenious a plan, and this from the only member of the group labeled "Gifted" by the Illinois state educational system.

Mike was voted the delivery guy. The rest of The Brothers would communicate with Brian via the walkie, keeping a safe distance from the neighbor Brian's home. One final touch was necessary. Before embarking on their late night escapade, the boys made Mike tiptoe back upstairs and scrounge up all the black clothes he could find, ski masks included. Hidden in black, The Brothers didn't have to walk far under the one or two streetlights. Brian's house was only two hundred feet from Mike's front door.

A palace guard of large oak and pine trees lined Brian's yard, giving the group of communicators much needed cover. Mike was feeling squeamish before setting out to his neighbor's. Although he had downed the last of the Michelob an hour before, he was surprisingly coherent.

"Where you guys going to be?" asked Mike. "For my retreat," he explained.

"We'll be waitin' for you behind them two trees right there," Doc assured him, pointing to the two girthy oaks standing about fifty feet to the side of Brian's house.

"If he comes out with his shotgun," Herb ribbed, "you better run like shit."

Assuming their positions, the boys readied themselves.

Stealthily, Mike approached Brian's front porch and cautiously placed the walkie at the foot of the door. Then he poked the doorbell and fled, jumping off the porch with the athleticism that would impress the college scouts one day and taking refuge with The Brothers who were aligning themselves in the streetlight shadow of the trees.

About a minute went by without so much as a candle flicker from the house. The boys hissed at Mike to try her again. It was as close to war as these boys would, thankfully, ever see, and the closer Mike got to the porch, the closer to reality the mission seemed. Mike's adrenaline kicked in, and this time he rang the doorbell not once but with multiple pecks, then split for the tree like a bat out of a belfry.

Again nothing. The pendulous leaves of the oak made aspirant sounds in the sweet November breeze of the night, which carried the scent of soybean dust swept off the harvested fields. A semi truck roared 'round the corner of Light and Swanwick in the distance, but Bobber felt no homesickness. He never did. In Chester, he was always home.

"This is gonna be a bust," he said, shaking his head. But there had been enough excitement this evening. He had been dunked on by an eighth-grader and made to walk home. They'd found the beer treasure, dropped off like a Mexican drug deal. Although he didn't much imbibe himself, he would kiss the fermented foam and make a tasty temporary mustache. Like the other boys, he just wanted to have fun, to feel important, and, a feeling he could only barely sense in the insulary time capsule that is teenage years, to become a man.

It wasn't like the boys to give up. They always thought of themselves as brave souls, braver as Brothers. Heroes often had one practical virtue that could be measured: persistence. How many times had this or that American war hero "repeatedly returned to the battlefield"! The Brothers decided to give it one last shot.

The third attempt saw the young hero slowly make his way back to the porch, as though through a minefield. Sensing something was about to happen, the always attentive Doc prophesied in a whisper, "This isn't going to be good."

The moment the skittish eighth-grader set foot on the porch, a strange image came into the peripheral view of The Brothers kneeling in the lookout area. The image they saw astounded them. The hair, the bod, the skivvies... a half-naked, 250-pound monster peaking around the back wall of the house.

"Holy shit!" It was Brian himself, debouched from his bed.

Mike was now about to be trapped on the porch. Before anyone could find his voice, the half-naked man in his undies let out the roar of a beast and charged the future football star. Mike broke from the porch before Brian could tackle him. Before anyone knew anything, Mike was bolting up Riverview Boulevard. The chase lasted only about two blocks before Mike outlasted the thirty-eight-year-old corrections officer and ducked into an alley. Riverview, the desolate side street on the south side of town, became a legendary escape route that fateful November eve.

The commotion of a small herd of buffalo calves scrambling into the Niermann yard woke up Linda. She quickly discerned the booze and the impropriety, but was gracious and understanding as always, even in her nightgown and bathrobe. Just as they thought they were going to get away with it, The Brothers saw the situation transform into a much more complicated matter.

Linda spotted her half-naked neighbor panting, half hunched over and trudging down Riverview.

"What's going on Brian? Are you okay?" Linda called.

"I … chased … some punk ass … kid up … street," Brian strained to explain. He came to the Neirmann's boundary and stopped, hunching over on his knees. "The li'l prick … knockin' on my door, then leavin'. Thought somebuddy tryin' to break in."

Linda put her hand on Brian's back. "Was it Michael?"

"I dunno," said Brian, straightening up. "Whoever it was they ran that way." He was pointing in the direction of Allen Place, the side street halfway up Riverview Boulevard.

The other four boys, adrenaline still pumping and working up quite a sweat, sat as innocent as possible on the porch, as though they had just finished evening prayers. When Brian finally exited the scene, a shadowy figure emerged from the woods behind the Niermann house.

It was Mike. He had run the entire distance of Riverview, across Allen Place, down Mill Street hill, and doubled back through the woods to his house. It had to have been over a mile. "GET OVER HERE RIGHT NOW

MICHAEL!" said Linda in a firm, angry voice. No general decked in full military honors could have been more imperious than Linda Niermann in bathrobe, in moonlight, ordering her son to the court-martial hearing. "You guys go inside," she told Bobber, Doc, Herb, and James, "I'll talk with you later."

The four could hardly hold it together descending the cold, linoleum stairs to the basement. "Mike is totally screwed," Doc studiously observed. But it did not take a "gifted" acumen to know this.

"Linda'll get over it," James assured everyone. And everyone there, sinking exhausted back onto the cocoon of his blanket, knew it was true. They all had a mom. If the dads of Chester made you walk home after a bad game, the moms made you stay at home. Mike was grounded for two weeks.

Reminiscing on the incredible successes of the night, The Brothers didn't sleep much. As proof of Forgiveness and Mercy, Linda's pancakes filled the morning Neirmann home like sunshine and incense.

Scarfing down sweet maple-soaked pancakes and bacon and thanking Linda for the sleepover, the boys departed each to his own home, deeply satisfied. How they would brag to their classmates for the rest of the year about the exploits of that forgivable, unforgettable night!

CHAPTER ELEVEN
Buds

"Damn." That about summed it up. "Look at the size of those guys," said Herb. He and Bobber on the first good spring day of 1996 had decided on the eighteen-mile pleasure ride up the prison road to Ellis Grove and back. As they rode their bikes on the road parallel the impenetrable iron fence of the state penitentiary, they slowed to observe inmates in orange prison jumpsuits out in the open air. The spring air sweeping in huge gusts must have felt to them as it felt to the boys, like a breath of freedom. It made you want to get on your bike and ride in the wind. For Bobber and Herb it would be a half hour against it paying off in a wind pushed bike ride back home. The prisoners got two hours a day in it.

"Shit," said Herb. "they lift weights all day long?" Even from the road, the men in comical, humiliating orange looked blocky and solid.

"I don't see how my dad does it, working in there around all that." Bobber couldn't fathom the mental hardness it took to work in the prison every day. The boys churned into the wind, their tee shirts blustering like sails. On the way home, it would propel them like two kites on wheels.

Later that night, as Sharon was laying out dinner, which included chicken tetrazzini, fresh cantaloupe, green beans, and what the boys called "legendary," her homemade rolls, Bobber asked his dad how the inmates got so big. Danny had grown almost numb to any discussion of his work at the prison. It seemed as if he didn't want any reminder of that place when he was home with his family.

"Well, son," he began reluctantly, "when you do heinous things, you get punished. The men in prison have done things that they have to suffer the consequences for. Most of their freedoms have been taken away from them. One of the freedoms they do have is an hour or two each day to take part in some form of recreation. It's up to them to decide how to spend that time. Some lift weights." After grace, and a stab at the chicken, Danny Ohlau returned, "You boys been working out, like I suggested you do?"

The spring of '96 marked the official end of grade school for the Smothers Brothers. They would graduate from eighth grade and, after a summer of baseball, head off to Chester High, the one set of brick buildings in town that was the long-term goal of every boy in town as much as the prison was the opposite. Friday nights in high school, people from all over town and in from the country poured into the stands for football games. There was no more pleasant evening in the early fall, when the crop was picked, than to sit back and relive in person, as it were, the memory of when you were young and loved contact and felt no hesitation at banging your body full steam against the toughest kids from the neighboring county in what amounted to mock warfare. There was no greater satisfaction than knocking a quarterback unconscious from the blind side. Now you could sit back and gain vicarious enjoyment watching your sons do the same.

Football was certainly the biggest spectator event in Chester when the weather in southern Illinois made for a fall evening so pleasant that even Gramma came out to sit in the stands and enjoy the padded brutality on the field. But no matter how close high school was in their future, and no matter how much they loved the contact, and the roar of the Chester townspeople in the only unison that a thousand people can make, and the whiff of Angus burgers grilling and the smell of popcorn on the air, and not a single person, not even the hog or dairy farmers smelling anything but good, The Brothers loved baseball more. They must have loved it. How many games they played in the sweltering heat of summer, when the aluminum of a lawn chair could burn a stripe on Gramma's leg before she could react and hardly anyone came to the games. Yes, high school and that first fall football game was a pleasant future thought.

But summer is the present glory. Spring in southern Illinois is an awakening. On a certain three day stretch in April, around Eastertime, colors bloom one day at a time in certain succession. First come the forsythia bushes, the gangly bright yellow harbingers of spring. Then the white Bartlett pear trees release a chemical odor that is like gardenia mixed with ammonia. You take it in with swift spurts of the nostril like a smelling salt. The whole tree turns pure white like the punch holes from 5-Star binder paper. Compared to the forsythia, the pear trees seem to have trimmed themselves. They're perfect. A pure white tree is a rare and beautiful sight. Then come the lilac bushes, whose corsagey blooms smell like grapes, and the redbuds, smallish trees the size of the pear trees but pink to lavender. Southern Illinois is so known for its redbuds there's even a town by that name. Yellow, white, pink— it's a three day stretch around Easter that makes the whole southern Illinois landscape look like an outdoor wedding.

But soon these ephemeral colors yield to summer which they are but the heralds of. Its heat is already upon you, and swimming pools open by Memorial Day in southern Illinois. Spring has been the warmup for baseball, but summer is the real thing, and the baseball cap that you screwed onto your head when the redbuds burst is now coming into its main purpose: shade for your eyes, so you don't lose a pop fly in the sun. For the summer, The Brothers usually messed around and shaved each other's heads—last year they had shaved MS + PP on Herb's head and left the Nike logo on Doc's—but this time around, they wanted something superior. They met at Uptown Barbershop where part-time barber and part-time Gilster truck driver Jeff Dillard had an old wooden TV that seemed to play nothing but *Golden Girls*. Within reach of the barber chair he had a gallon jug of tea, and a lit cigarette both of which he sipped from all day. He exhaled tea flavored smoke along with his recommendations into the face of each of The Brothers while he examined their hair. One by one they took their seat to have it all buzzed off, as though they had been drafted. Baseball haircuts—for the immediate concern of The Brothers were two: how they would not merely tolerate the hot summer but look distinguished in it and how their baseball team could repeat as Class "A" National Champs.

The team that was returning for the encore was identical to the one that won Nationals the year before with the exception of two things. The boys were now much bigger, and the coaching staff was different.

As Danny Ohlau had recommended, the weight room at Chester High, now available to incoming athletes, became the new club for the buzz-cut Brothers, that and Program 1, the new gym in town, a two-mile bike ride away. "Chicks dig the long ball," was their motto for the summer, as they inched the bench press pin higher and higher—laughing all summer at the time Dave Milby had somehow smashed his penis in the weights the year before.

"Wouldn't even hurt me," they bragged.

"Milby can marry a virgin," they laughed.

Whether the boys were pumping iron, pretending to be convicts or pro football players, goofing around outside on Doc's patio basketball court attempting to grab the rim and the attention of the eighth grade beauty, Jess, who lived next door, or riding bikes out to Program 1, the boys were relishing in an element of summer youth they had heretofore only feigned: testosterone. Would it translate to a repeat performance in the Nationals? The bench press pins inched up.

"Won't... hurt... me," The Brothers laughed and groaned.

. . . . .

For whatever reason—maybe they just didn't feel like taking it on—Gary, The Sheriff, and Big Bruce decided not to coach the Juvenile II's in the summer of '96. Instead, three 19-year-olds, only recently graduated high school upstarts, wanted the job.

Coach Beaver, a nickname he earned from unmentionable rumors, was a recent CHS graduate and former starting catcher from the high school team. He had enrolled at Southeast Missouri State University with the intention of walking on. "They needed a bullpen catcher," Beave shrugged. "They still cut me."

But that hadn't stymied his love for baseball. He volunteered as head coach of the Juveniles, his friends Dave and Brett to assist him.

Dave, known as "The Maaaan" to the boys, was the more laid back of the three. Dave said very little in the form of coaching during practices but proved to be a great practical asset, hurling numerous rounds of batting practice, as well as hitting countless balls to the infielders.

This was not the authoritarianism of Sheriff Peters and Warden Gary Knop from the previous year. This was different, much different. The boys had no problem with the fun-loving young men taking over the team. Getting away from parental hovering was freeing to the boys. The only rules they felt they needed were the rules of the game.

There was structure, however. Practices were structured after pre-game rituals in the major leagues. Defensive work would take up the first part of the practice while hitting ended it. After a few of these practices, Beaver and Dave quickly found out the challenges of coaching that preceded any glory.

"I need a beer," the 19-year-old Beaver would say after most practices. He was getting exhausted.

"You oughta quit drinking both before *and* after," Dave suggested, but none too critically.

"How 'bout the kids throw BP to each other instead of us doing it all the time?" Beave said, hunched over. He decided to build a portable backstop out of two-by-fours and a tarp from the Gilsters' supply room where he worked just so he wouldn't have to walk so far picking up stray baseballs. He attached wheels to it to cart it on and off the field.

"Where the hell did you get that?" Meat asked, scowling at the contraption. "Did you find it at the dump?"

Though shoddy, the Portable Beave Backstop actually made a huge difference. As the failed bullpen catcher turned youth baseball coach hurled batting practice balls, the balls that missed bats plopped directly into the tarp. Beave had once watched a cricket game at the campus of Southeast Missouri State. No backstop there and players walked after the ball. "No wonder that damn game takes three days to play," Beave complained.

"Wow, it actually works," the boys laughed, trying to throw fastballs to knock over Beave's contraption like a State Fair carnival game.

Practices went on like this all spring and into the early summer, as the Juveniles were racking up wins. They boasted a record of 14–0 leading into the weekend tournament before districts. Beave continued to drink both before and after the games and practice.

The fact that they were undefeated mattered to the boys, but it wasn't the sole desideratum of the parents. Parental questions and concerns came and went like chirping birds in the small town during the summer of '96.

"Was Beaver a bad influence on the boys?"

"Has he been drunk during practices?"

"I heard Herb and James almost drowned in the Mississippi one night after practice … an entire case of Budweiser."

"They'll end up getting somebody killed."

"The backs of their trucks are ballast with beer cans."

"Fred and Gary should take back the team."

In a small town, the kernel of a truth could be added to and fermented into something sour enough to act upon. It was as much a sign of true concern as of the importance of baseball that a parent's meeting was held at Chester City Hall on the night of July 12. On the agenda was one item: getting rid of the coaches.

"NO KIDS ALLOWED," read the sign before the chambers of City Hall. The boys knew, however, what was being talked about on the other side of the door. They had come to City Hall—the smallish brick building, derivative of something in Washington, D.C., but with a copper barn cupola on top advertising an image of Popeye. It sufficed for town meetings. The boys sat outside on the steps, waiting to learn not just the coaches' fate but their own.

"You know if Beaver and Dave wouldn't show up to practice drinking and getting you guys beer, we all wouldn't be here right now," said Peters, scowling at the underclassmen teammates. He was physically the most mature of the group and his severe Nordic features coupled with a meanness that regularly animated his brows made him look like an outlaw from an Old West Wanted poster.

"Dude, we don't need Beaver to coach us," Meat contended. The largest boy on the team, Meat was the only one who could stand up to Peters. "We could win with anybody coachin'. Shit, Beaver was passed out on the bench last game."

Every member of the team, including The Brothers, knew that the coaches' behavior was inappropriate, but the young men who made up the Juvenile II's didn't care; they enjoyed the attention. A City Hall town meeting had been called on their behalf!

If Beaver's indiscretions amounted to the

misdirecting of minors, it wasn't in the area of baseball that he was guilty. His portable backdrop was making batting practice more productive than it had ever been. And he treated the boys like men that summer of '96.

There was a heated exchange echoing inside the city council's chambers on this night. "I'll crush his skull!" yelled The Sheriff as the parents discussed Beaver's fate.

"I say we disband the team," The Warden motioned. "It's evident that Beaver can't handle himself. He should be arrested."

"Now, let's not get crazy," Danny Ohlau stood up and owing to the respect he commanded with his quiet nature, the crowd of parents calmed down enough to hear him out. "When things get like this in my home there is one thing that I do. I take a step back, take a deep breath, and cool my thoughts. We should all do that at this time."

A few quieter moments later, the meeting adjourned, the parents grimly made their way out of the double doors of the conference room. The town council had heard enough. They would now vote.

Danny Ohlau shepherded Bobber out to the car. It was time to go home. They would find out the decision later.

CHAPTER TWELVE
Hallandale

"Tíralo al hombre cortado!"
"What'd he say?" asked Meat.
"He said he wants mustard on his hot dog."

The answer from the town council rang tinnily but clear enough the following day. A recycling stash of Budweiser beer cans rattling in the bed of the red Dodge Dakota, Beaver and Dave pulled up to Cohen Field #2 to the cheers of the boys. And there was another, more beautiful aluminum sound rattling in the bed: baseball bats.

The team needed a good practice. They had experienced their first loss of the season to a team that was quickly becoming their arch rival, the Juvies from Belleville. That, most thought, was the real reason Beave and Dave were on probation. After the mid-summer drama that had brought all the adults to the place where disputes were settled, the town hall, it was time for the boys to settle matters of their own. The baseball field was their court of law. They needed to get back to playing ball and forget all of that which everyone else wanted to control.

Beave threw the bag of bats down like a gauntlet. "Let's go, men!" Bobber and Mike went to roll out the backstop. Even if their two coaches were being closely monitored by Mr. Lochead, the new President of Chester Sports, it was the freedom summer of '96 to them. "Let's go, boys!" called Dave, clapping his hands smartly. Juvenile II was going for a repeat national championship.

The team, on the back of a five home run day from Meat and Peters in their regular season finale, once again qualified for Class "A." After all they had been through, they were extremely optimistic about their chances in the upcoming tournament.

Districts proved to be little challenge for the Juveniles, as they rolled through Valier, a team from a little town in the heart of southern Illinois, population 669. Chester beat Valier 3–1 and 16–2 en route to an easy tournament win and a birth in the state tourney.

State, however, was a different story. Being held in the town of Mascoutah, only thirty miles from St. Louis, it allowed for the best metro area teams to participate. It was one thing to beat puny Valier, quite another to take on the spoiled suburban city slickers of St. Louis, home of the National League's greatest dynasty, the Cardinals.

Chester was not favored to win. Coming off an impressive win versus the defending National Champions a couple weekends prior and playing on a field almost in their own backyard, the Belleville team was seeded higher. They had dominated in the summer of 1996. The county seat, with 40,000 citizens, Belleville, Illinois, maintained one of the longest running Khoury league participants in the entire country. They had the nice uniforms to prove it. Every year Belleville carried a select roster loaded with future high school stars and even draft picks.

The East St. Louis Bulls rounded out the tourney. No slouches themselves, the Bulls were fast, athletic, and raw. Beaver knew if his team was going to repeat as National Champs, getting through State was going to be their first huge challenge.

With hard-fought wins over the Bulls and Belleville in the first two games of the tournament, the Juvies faltered, losing to Belleville in Game One of the Championship Series. Out of pitching, the Juvies turned to another one of their lefties to carry them to Nationals.

The unlikely hero of the day was Doc. Never one to back down from a challenge, Doc nudged his glasses tight on the bridge of his nose and took the mound for his first start of the season. He pitched like a man possessed as his mom, Marsha, and his Grandpa Willie hollered from the stands.

"Throw 'em that old dark one, Matt!" screamed Willie.

"Strike 'em out, Matt!" yelled Marsha. Doc seemed to thrive at the sound of his real name. The veins in his bull neck bulged each time he reared back to fire a pitch at Meat's demanding mitt. No one yelled louder than Peters and Bobber whose pitching arms were recovering.

But with all the noise coming from Doc's camp, one voice was silent, absent. Doc's dad was back in the hotel room a mile down the road, still drunk from the night before. "At least he's there," said Sharon Ohlau, setting up her lawn chair and putting the best construction on everything. At least Doc had a dad.

Beaver didn't say much either that game. He sat quietly on the bench with a similar ailment—the Chester bug—while Dave handled things on the field. Doc allowed six runs on seven hits during his 6 1/3 innings of work, a driven, almost angry performance against one of the best Khoury League teams in the entire country. Chester scored twice as many runs to back him up.

Chester prevailed 12–8, and again were Class "A" State Champs. With the team now 25–2 on the season, a remarkable record but nothing beyond expectations, Beave's captainship was secure. The worst he brought to games and practice were *empty* beer cans and a hangover. But there was one more job to be done before full exoneration. The Juveniles were once again headed to the elusive Class "A" National Tournament.

This year, Nationals would be held in Wright City, Missouri, a town a full two hours from their little river city. Several of the boys had never even been that far away from home before. Their opponent, however, was from much farther away, farther than any of The Brothers could have imagined.

Top Row L-R: Coach Brett, Knop, Luthy, Peters, Niermann, Meat,
Coach Dave, Coach Beave
Bottom Row L-R: Zach, Bobber, Herb, Phil, Doc, Rainman

•   •   •   •   •

"Tíralo al hombre cortado!" yelled the Hallandale coach
as he hit in and out to his team of young teenagers.

"What'd he say?" asked Meat, standing on the top
step of the dugout at the National Championship field.

"He said he wants mustard on his hot dog." Meat
looked to see if Doc was joking.

In 1996, Hallandale Beach, Florida, was one of the
fastest growing cities in Broward County. Of
Hallandale's citizens, only 80% spoke English as their
first language, 20% spoke Spanish.

"Todo el Camino!"

The Chester boys watched, almost perplexed, as the
game they knew so well was translated into a different

language. The bright uniforms of the Hallandale Hots, their bronze skin, the grace in the way they scooped up grounders and threw to first with an arch of the back, the throwing arm describing a perfect half circle— stopped you and made you question for the first time in your life whether your dads had taught you right.

South Florida, where baseball could be played 365 days a year, produced some of the best high school and college programs in the United States. Their Khoury League was no exception.

Chester beat the Marlins from Fort Lauderdale, Florida, to advance to the National Championship game on July 27, 1996. But they had never experienced an opponent like Hallandale before. Living in the bubble of their secluded, little riverbank town in Illinois, they had thought Spanish was only spoken in foreign countries and manufacturing plants, not on baseball fields in Wright City and definitely not by any opponent of theirs. The two teams vying for the year's crown of best in Class "A" couldn't have come from more opposite parts of the country. No matter the differences, one thing was for certain, each loved playing the game of baseball.

"Todo el Camino, no lo rebote." It was clear to the Juvies that this was not their ordinary opponent. These guys were good-very good all over the field. And none of them spoke a lick of English. Were the stories true? Were these kids brought to America just to play baseball?

El Camino? The only *el Camino* The Brothers knew

was the one they had sloshed around in the metal bed of, an orange '69 El Camino, driven by some sixteen-year-old farmboy who knew how to peel out and turn the gravel backroads of Chester, spitting gravel.

Most of the teams the Juvies had encountered throughout the course of a summer had a good core of players but with a right fielder or second baseman who was tacked on. Hallandale was different. They were rock solid at every position. Select teams can be this way.

Beave hadn't exactly been forthcoming about the Spaniards of Hallandale prior to everyone's arrival in Wright City. But the boys had read the National Championship program when they got there.

"Four national titles?" Doc's mouth dropped.

Peters, followed by Meat, scoffed. That didn't mean shit.

But as they watched their opponents warm up, Chester noted how the graceful Hallandale fielders fielded the ball with a softness that only comes from years of love of the game and practice. But what stood out most was the camaraderie among their teammates. Theirs too was a brotherhood. Their style, their desire, their oneness. It stood out. Their language. They were special. "It almost seemed in a way like we were playing ourselves," Bobber would years later observe. "I think it scared us."

Hallandale's lead-off man swung the bat like he was special. He slipped the batting doughnut off with a rhythmic tap to the ground, a mechanical efficiency — a

St. Louis Chrysler assembly line worker couldn't have slipped a washer on a bolt any slicker. *These boys can play*, Chester realized, even before one of them stepped into the batter's box.

The only comment Bobber on the mound heard from his new enemies, the only thing he could make out was "Nada." This guy has *nada*.

The boys from South Florida were only not entirely incorrect in their assessment of Southern Illinois. Chester struggled to get anything going in the championship series versus the Hots from Hallandale. "Hit it where they ain't!" Beave cried, countering the indecipherable Spanish from the opposite dugout. Baseball is the common language of American youth and is spoken in many different ways. The rougher looking Chester boys were not outmatched that day — but seemed to be out-lucked. They answered the arch-backed spit fire of the Hallandale ace with pings from new aluminum bats, but no matter what came flying off the Chester bats, there seemed to be a Hot waiting. Was it their skill? Or was it the baseball gods? In the end for Chester — nada.

With strong pitching and exceptional defense, the team from Hallandale ended the Chester Juvenile II's dream of a second consecutive National Title and ultimately The Brother's Khoury league career.

"Keep your heads up," called the Chester dads as their sons lined up to touch hands with the boys from Hallandale, and when they looked up they were surprised. The boys from Hallandale looked them in the eyes, with dark brown eyes, and told them in clear English, "You guys played a great game." No one had ever in victory used complete sentences.

It was a sign of respect.

The Chester Juveniles after the Hallandale game

Back Row L-R: Coach T.K. ("Beave"), Coach Dave, Michael Niermann, Bruce Luthy, Phil Grau, Matt "Doc" Davitz, Zach Engel
Front Row L-R: Craig "Bobber" Ohlau, Matt "Herb" Seymour, Jarrod Peters, James "Rainman" Knott, Adam "Meat" Gibbs, Michael Knop

. . . . .

After the Hallandale loss, the future seemed unclear for the group of friends who had ended their junior high careers and were anticipating high school. Times were changing, new friends were forming, and girls began dominating their thoughts. Nonetheless, they entered Chester High School with dreams of greatness. As they entered that August the world of young *men*, the world of high school, one dream in particular was growing in their minds. In some ways, it was greater even than the national championship they had won a year earlier. This dream was to be achieved not among boys but among men. It was to win the Illinois High School State Championship.

PART THREE:
DREAM SEASON

CHAPTER THIRTEEN
"Bobber is dead!"

There he sat, aching on the old white couch in the family living room, face red, throat dry, and knee throbbing from the six-mile early morning run. High school cross country practice was so different than baseball. Why did they have to run in the *morning*, anyway? Bobber always loved running, almost as much as riding his bike, and it always came easy to him. In junior high he had almost broken the five-minute mile barrier—an accomplishment that seemed the equivalent of the great Jim Ryan, the first high schooler ever to do it, breaking the *four*-minute mile barrier. Now, however, Bobber couldn't even make it to the kitchen and back on those legs. When he stood up to go get a drink out of the faucet, he found himself barely even capable of limping the twenty feet to the sink. He struggled his way into the bathroom, searching for something to dull the pain. "1000 mg Tylenol," he read on the bottle.

Bobber was now fifteen years old, a sophomore, his bones growing rapidly. His right knee, which had always given him problems since a football incident down in St. Mary's Bowl as a youngster, was now in more pain than ever. The pressures that a young man puts on himself for high school sports were mounting. In a small school, the boys who excel and obtain scholarships, Bobber knew, succeed early in their high school careers, breaking records and winning championships. "Old people are the ones with knee problems," he muttered at the bathroom mirror.

The nagging injuries and pressures that were plaguing him were taking as great a toll on his psyche. In two years he would be graduating and either heading off to college or forced to get a job. It was a reality the security of a good father and family had forestalled for as long as possible. But "real life," a matter his dad had often alluded to by name, was now coming into view. He longed to hold onto his high school days, but when was over he wanted college. An athletic scholarship. That other option just scared him.

As he hobbled back to the couch, he caught a glimpse of the headline on the sports page of the Herald Tribune: "Football Looking for Strong Year." He felt keenly the narrowing hope of his time in high school and the importance of making every day count. The upcoming sports season, with half the town congregating in the stands on a crisp Friday night, seemed like somebody else's dream. He was putting in lonely miles on country roads, no one in sight, and his knee was killing him. The world that awaited him, the one that Danny and Sharon spent so much time over the years preparing him for, was exciting and scary and suddenly becoming very real. With his buddies on the gridiron, and he laid up with a bum leg, unsure of what the basketball season might bring, he seemed lost.

One night in the fall of their freshman year, Doc and Bobber were sitting on the roof of the porch at Light and Swanwick, enjoying the view. Bobber was dangling his bum leg. The two got to talking about a party they had gone to and how some of the older high school seniors — The Goons — were harassing Zach and Bobber for not drinking the booze.

"I don't give a shit who's saying stuff to us. I don't care if it's the captain of the football team or anybody," Bobber told Doc. The Nordic stubbornness that must have come over with the Vikings some centuries ago took many forms, some of them good.

"Ya," said Doc quietly.

"Z should have felt the same," Bobber said. He knew all about "leading by example," a phrase probably invented by Scandinavians, who not only led the way to America but were naturally taciturn.

The boys dangled their legs off the porch for a time. The view from the top of the Ohlau house was, if not beautiful, commanding. They could see the trucks coming around the corner from afar and the Gilster chute down the street and listen for the sounds of traffic slipping along the Mississippi.

Then Doc said quietly, "I wish I could be more like you."

•   •   •   •   •

With high school, of course, came temptations beyond quenching your thirst. There were new thirsts. Maybe it was the sentiment of missing out on football, the idea that life was short, even *quick*, or simply the fact that Joni was a cute, older cheerleader with a car, that drew him to her. She talked quick, had a bubbly personality, was blonde (he loved blonde) and had a kind heart, and seemed to always live in the moment. These blinding qualities for a few weeks that fateful fall, obscured his vision of the future. He couldn't even see down the road — quite literally on the night of September 5, 1998.

Saturday nights in Chester were nights of mystery. An old timer might look twice on the road and thought to have seen high school boys and girls swimming in the bed of a pickup truck. The makeshift, portable skinny-dipping pool was as easy to come by as following simple instructions: lay a tarp in the back, drive to the water plant, for seventy-five cents fill the bed with water. If you were lucky, you might get a couple bikinis in there. Paintball battles were common, even between moving cars. Booze cruising down the Chester strip was practically a tradition. Barn wrestling often followed.

Barn wrestling — no one can be sure when it started but Chester, Illinois, in an old barn a mile south of town is as good a provenance as any. There, the sons of Chester built a genuine wrestling ring in the heart of the barn. For half a generation before, Quonset huts all over the Midwest were collapsing like discarded tin cans and broken back barns began to rot for want of the one thing that had kept their temperatures warm in the winter: cattle and hogs. The boycotts of the Carter administration and the campaigns against red meat ("Pork, the other white meat" had been one of the ingenious slogans of the Illinois Pork Growers) and the lure of engineering jobs in Denver and Dallas left farms bereft not only of livestock but of hands to feed them. The vacancy at the old barn was filled in the mid-90s by The Brothers. There, where straw for hog bedding and hay for cattle feed had once been piled in bales that built the scratched forearms of three generations of farmboys, they built a wrestling ring.

It was a fair facsimile of what they had seen on the videos. There on a Friday or Saturday night, the Impala and the pickup trucks, some still sloshing with tarp contained pool water, and a Chevy and Malibu or two would park on the rough concrete once trodden by the cloven hooves of market swine, and teenage boys and girl spectators would meet in the barn for the wildest romp in the hay the Midwest had seen in two generations—the southern Illinois version of Wrestlemania! Things got pretty wild. Two of the gamest boys would strip off their shirts and take to the ring, its mat of raised plywood covered by two thick paint tarps. It had a nice spring to it so that a fireman's takedown or jump off the top rope—thick hemp rope string square between four fence posts, with turnbuckles—or a grab your opponent by the ankles and swing him around like a discus thrower would only knock the wind out of you. Spectators lined the ring and slapped on the tarp and hooted from the barn rafters above that a hundred years earlier had been hewn from white oak trees on the very property and fitted together by mortise and tenon joints.

One time when he was twelve, in the barn on the Ohlau farm, Bobber had climbed up to one of the rafters — in order to jump. The straw from some 4-H fair calf or Yorkshire hog long ago shown and butchered lay in thin remembrance 18 feet below. Bobber stood up to jump. There was just something about that barn beam, so natural and artistic as a tree whittled down to a structural element by a man, that called him. Rough hewn and wide enough to stand up on comfortably and grayed for a century and still retaining the dusty musty hay smell of the barn and the smell of farm animals faintly, the barn beam called. Then he looked down and saw it.

Whittled by some very sharp knife on the top of the beam, the name of his grandfather. Hmm, thought Bobber. Every other generation an Ohlau boy gets it in his head to jump 18 feet from a barn beam. He jumped and was surprised at how long it took him to hit the barn floor.

Perhaps that launch into history and gravity had something to do with his bad knee. He couldn't be sure. When Lindbergh landed in Paris, for sure he had no regrets of the toll it had taken on his psyche. When Neil Armstrong bounced on the face of the moon, all the long trip was worth it. When Bobber landed, as his grandfather had landed, there was no less sense of accomplishment. Then he recalled that Grampa Ohlau also had a limp...

In the summer you played whiffle ball in the barnyard,

and the barn was like a stadium. Hit the barn door—a double. On the roof—a home run, but the fielder still had a chance to catch the white ball with holes before it hit the ground. Over the barn—grand slam. Bobber held in memory not a few dramatic moments playing whiffle ball on the farm.

Inside the barn, the Gambrel rafters and the two-tiered hay loft and beams and the walls that no storm in a century could blow down and the great sliding barn door a hay wagon could fit through and the chewed pens that once held hogs and the dust that stirred with each body slam made the barn the greatest gymnasium. No wonder they used to call a close and chaotic fourth quarter basketball game a "barn burner." Hood the horses, un-pen the cattle and hogs, and run for your life, chickens! The barn is on fire! To the rafters rose cheers from the teens as they watched Herb, the bodybuilder who had eaten nothing but chicken and popsicles in grade school to prepare his physique, battle Doc. It was a great match—Herb twirling Doc in a helicopter hold at one point and the rest of The Brothers jumping into the ring to join in. Once in a while they tossed in a girl. It was a wonder that this activity never got the sanction of the Illinois High School Athletic Association.

But on this particular Saturday night, September 5, 1998, things would not turn out so much fun.

. . . . .

Although The Smothers Brothers had unofficially disbanded due to high school pressures stressing individuality, they continued to remain close. A phone call from Mike marked the beginning of one fateful evening. A born prankster and expert storyteller, Mike ate up the high school lifestyle. He was very popular with the upper classmen and wasn't afraid to have a few drinks, hanging with the best of them.

But Bobber, who had never acquired the taste for beer, on this quiet late summer's eve wanted only to embrace life. He didn't need to be thinking of his leg injury nor of the upcoming basketball season, which held the hope that he and his real blood brother, Jason, who was now a senior, would lead the Yellow Jackets to their first regional title since their father had done it twenty-three years earlier.

"How about we just go to Joni's and watch a movie or something? You bring Lindsey. I'm sure we'll end up doing something after the movie anyways." Bobber told Mike. Although the two boys had a long history of foolish endeavors, they needed a quiet night with the girls, the kind of evening that Bobber had seen in its married form from his mom and dad, who watched TV shows together, with a quiet and long-tested understanding between them.

Joni was the upper classwoman whom Bobber had been hanging out with of late, the bubbly one. The fact that Joni had a car was an added incentive. Anytime they needed to go somewhere, she was more than willing to take them. She picked up the entire crew and headed to Ellis Grove, a small village nine miles north of Chester, where she called home.

The night started off as planned. The four hung out in the living room of the ranch-style home, watching *Scream*, the modern horror classic. Bobber and Mike listened to the girls scream until around 11:00 p.m.

"Let's go to the stilt houses," Mike suggested when the screaming was over. The girls reluctantly agreed, and the four piled into Joni's red Chevy hatchback.

"You guys know the stilt houses are haunted, right?" Mike reminded them. No one needed reminding of that. Everyone knew that Ku Klux Klan meetings were held out there and that someone was even murdered in one of those houses.

"He was hung from the big oak tree in the yard," Bobber said, reciting the local legend. "In front of the third house, and didn't die from the hangin'. He hung for *hours*, blowin' in the wind before they blew him away with buck shot."

Bobber put his foot on top of Joni's over the accelerator. "Let's go," he whispered in her ear.

The stilt houses are houses located in the river bottom near the village. The cabins themselves are used mostly for deer hunting. They were built on stilts thirty or so years prior, designed against flooding. Myths and legends surrounded the mysterious shacks, and they became a popular weekend destination for teenage mischief. The boys were more than excited to go check them out. Having girls with you — now that emboldened them.

To this day, depending on whom you ask about what happened on that dark, back country road, the details and stories remain a little fuzzy. The group set out with the best of intentions. Bobber slid in tight next to Joni who drove. In the back, Mike and Lindsey clung to each other. Bobber had won a zoo of stuffed animals for Joni with his pitching—at the county fair, and the collection of animals rode along in the back. With the midnight sky and gleaming stars providing the perfect back drop for a night of cruising in the Grove back country, Tom Petty's "Free Falling" blared out on the radio, and the four sang along. Joni, known for her skills on the gymnastic mat and not for the ones behind the wheel, seemed to be doing all right on this night. The Tom Petty classic had just reached its guitar playing climax three-fourths of the way into the song. Was it a deer? A coon? The fact that the car was traveling 40 miles per hour on loose gravel? Was it the turn in the road? It all still remains fuzzy.

"Hit the brakes," Mike said quickly, and the mood turned. Joni applied a little more brake than she should have. As soon as the old Chevy started to make the turn, the brakes locked as the sports car began fish tailing off the side of the road. Over correcting, Joni tried forcing the car back onto the road. This only compounded the problem. The car slid and eventually flipped over onto its side, ramming into the ditch on the righthand side of the road and coming to a sudden stop. The inside of the hatchback was a human pinball machine. In the freedom of the night, no one had buckled up.

When the dust cleared, the car was flipped on its side in the ditch of the country road.

"Is everyone okay?" called Mike.

The steering wheel had kept Joni from hitting the windshield while the back seats and, Mike would swear, the stuffed animals, protected him and Lindsey. Looking at Bobber's lifeless body in the front seat, limp against the passenger's side door no one knew what to do.

"Oh, my God, Bobber is dead!" cried out Lindsey, struggling to climb out of the overturned car.

"Bobber's not dead?" Mike cried defiantly.

With tears rolling down their faces, the girls sat on the side of the road trying to comprehend what had just happened. "Bobber is dead!" "O-my-God, O-my-God! I've never seen a dead body."

"Wake up, dude," Mike demanded the corpse. He was more a soldier than a priest, but somehow it worked.

"Give me your hand," Mike said to his Brother. "Ah ha, you are alive."

Dazed and confused, Bobber obeyed, grabbed the hand, and was pulled out of the broken car.

"Thank God you're not dead," Joni wept, hugging her beat up boyfriend. "My leg! It's probably broken!" she suddenly realized.

Mike was the only one with his full senses. "Bobber just had his head go through the windshield, and you're complainin' about your stupid leg."

The four limped as a group down the side of the starlit road. They knew they were extremely lucky, as none of them seemed to have any serious injuries other than maybe a slight fracture and Bobber's concussion. They made their way down the dark back road in the middle of the night in search of a house where they could use a telephone.

Not really understanding what was wrong with him other than the fact his head was hurting like crazy, and he couldn't remember a thing about what had just happened, Bobber figured they should get to the hospital as quickly as they could. After walking for half an hour on the quiet, romantic road, the group stumbled across an old farmhouse that didn't appear to be haunted. Lindsey, Bobber noticed as his thoughts cleared slightly, was still holding one of the teddy bears.

"They better be home," Mike said. It was dark, but there were cars in the driveway. The boys decided it would be best for them to knock gently on the door just in case a dog or shotgun greeted them. Mike put four knocks onto the old wooden door.

"Ma'am, we need to use your phone," Mike told the woman who tentatively answered the door. "We were in a car accident about a mile down the road, and we are pretty banged up."

"Someone ran us off the road," Joni added.

Instead of calling an ambulance, Joni decided to call her dad. His Silverado extended cab proved faster than any ambulance. Lindsey and Mike sat in the back while Joni sat with Bobber in the front. Barely able to keep his eyes open, neither caring nor comprehending where they were going or what was going on, Bobber slowly dozed off. Mike, from the back seat kept asking, "You okay, Bobber?"

When he awoke, Joni was helping him out of the truck as they slowly walked into Memorial Hospital's Emergency Room in Chester.

As the group entered the cold hospital waiting room, a nurse was first to greet them.

"We have been in a car accident," Mike told the nurse. The nurse immediately informed the emergency room doctor and other staff on duty. Bobber felt a cold stethoscope on his bare chest.

Mike volunteered to call Sharon and Danny Ohlau to let them know exactly just what the boys had encountered. The clock had just reached one in the morning. The two were supposed to be home two hours ago.

Sharon, notoriously vigilant in waiting up for her boys on nights like these, had already been phoning about town for the whereabouts of her son. The last place she wanted to phone was the hospital.

It took only half a ring for her to answer. "Sharon?" Mike said.

"Yes," Sharon replied, bracing herself.

"Now don't get mad at us or worried when I tell you this but Bobber and I were in a car accident tonight, and we are at the emergency room, and Bobber is getting a CAT scan on his head, but he is good, really good."

Sharon had held her breath until she heard "good." She let out a sigh she'd been holding in for two hours. It was 2 a.m. three hours past Bobber's curfew, but, she realized, it was Sunday.

At the hospital, Sharon and Dan barely recognized their middle son lying there on the bed in a hospital gown, his head swollen. The ER doc quickly assured them that there was no fluid on the brain. "He was extremely lucky," the doctor said.

But Sharon knew better. She had been praying for her son since 11 p.m. when he didn't come home.

Relieved that Craig would be alright, Danny turned his attention to causes. Who actually had been driving the car that careened off the road nearly killing his son?

He had already asked Mike, but now he geared the question towards Bobber. "So who was driving the car?" he asked quietly. Squinting from the bright lights of the emergency room Bobber replied, "The curly blonde. I think." Things were still fuzzy. "It wasn't me, was it?"

Discharged around 3:00 a.m., Bobber rode the two blocks home in complete silence. Quickly falling asleep in his bed, he woke up a quick seven hours later to find his mom standing over him like an angel. She hadn't slept.

A pounding headache, his hand in a cast, scabs crusting on his swollen head, a sore neck and bruises on most of his body—it didn't matter. "You get up and get ready for church," his mom said softly. It was Sunday.

Bobber hobbled the one block to St. Mary's. Mike was already there, waiting for him in the church balcony. The hospital was two blocks away, the church one. That had always seemed a safe symmetry to Sharon. The boys loved hearing the weekly renditions of Sue Reiman's "Ode to Joy," "Amazing Grace," or

"City of God" from the balcony organ, but on this day, a little peace and quiet was all they coveted. "A-MAZE-zing GRACE, how SWEEeeeT the SOUND!" Bobber's head throbbed with every note.

Grace. It throbbed in his temples. He had knelt down to pray as he entered the pew, and spoken in his heart, *Our Father who art in heaven, hallowed be thy name, thy kingdom come ..."* finishing with an equally fervent, *"O Lord, please let me heal before baseball."*

CHAPTER FOURTEEN
To Do It As Men

It was February 1, 1999. The car accident was a distant memory, and the dismal high school basketball season was about to come to a close. No one was more eager for the warm weather and sunshine heralding the beginning of the baseball season than Bobber, Jarrod, and the rest of the baseball team.

After a shitty start to sophomore year, and the disappointing regional loss to conference rival Du Quoin, forward thinking needed to prevail. Puberty and whatever chemicals it naturally worked in the minds and bodies of teenage boys stimulated by countless hours in the weight room were adding up to what could be a promising spring for the boys.

Lying in bed on the night of February 28, the night before the first practice of the season, Bobber could only dream of destroying some of the pitchers he would face this season, getting the game-winning hit, dominating opposing hitters from the mound, and doing it all over and over again. He imagined that if his high school had a record book, he could break every hitting and pitching record in it, earn a good scholarship to a university, and maybe just maybe, parlay that into a pro career that would eventually lead to a big league call-up. He never dreamed of anything but that. The curly blonde was no longer in his thoughts. The vision he remembered as early as age three when he first pretended to be the latest major league star in his parents two-room basement apartment had matured with him. But that element of reality that is dream is timeless. Young boys and old men on their deathbed, he imagined, all felt the same way.

The boys had talked about it constantly. They had talked about it during basketball, while hunting deer in the fall, while four wheeling in the Chester countryside, in the halls at school, and even while drinking beer in their cars cruising the Chester strip. Theirs was a single unifying goal: Do just as they did in Metropolis three years ago. Go all the way and win the whole, entire thing. Win the state championship. Be the best team in the heart of the heart of the nation, Illinois.

The town that was *foot*ball crazy had never seen the high school team even win a regional in baseball. But the sons of Chester now believed they could make history and put baseball on the map in the town that was known for its gridiron game.

Yellow forsythia bushes bloomed early and gangly against the white aluminum siding of homes in Chester that spring, the first outdoor color since Christmas decorations had been taken down. Baseball season was finally here. The excitement surrounding the start of the spring season seemed to be confined to the members of the team and the dads who saw in every spring newness of life. No one else in town seemed to be talking of baseball. That was fine with the boys. They were well aware baseball didn't draw the crowds that football and basketball did. Not even the local sports writers whose job it was to stir up interest seem much jubilant.

"Productive Offense Will Help Yellow Jackets Be Competitive in '99 Season," The headline of the spring sports preview in the *Chester Herald* read, rather underwhelmingly.

"Competitive?" spat Bobber. "That's for losers. Shouldn't it have said something about winning conference or making a trip to state? Damn it, we are going be good!" He pounded his fist into his glove. There was only one thing the team needed to do to earn the respect they all sought, and that was win.

Coach Jeff Kordys would be entering his sixth season as coach of the Yellow Jacket baseball team. His career 58–56 record was more indicative of the school's general lack of interest in baseball than it was in his understanding of the game. A commanding presence in pinstripes, Kordys had been a good ballplayer in his day, good enough for college, and his body in retirement, like that of every man in Chester was sturdy and constituted of pork and beer and now gave new contour about the waist to the Yellow Jacket pinstripes. He looked managerial, his high full cheeks shining with a bruised red color from days unprotected on the third base line. When he spoke, his words were crisp and precise, and he looked the boys in the eyes with the certainty that he knew something they didn't.

The previous year was Kordys's best finish, the team losing that heartbreaker to Du Quoin in the regional championship. Now, with much of the team returning from the year before, Coach Kordys was all optimism. He knew he had only four seniors, but they were all starters returning from the previous year.

Perhaps most importantly was his knowledge of the boys. The man had coached the group of boys throughout grade school. He had watched them grow up. He knew their talent but most important, he knew their dream. The authoritative but laid-back leader knew that if certain things came into place, the season could turn magical.

As the '99 season began, the Jackets were nowhere to be found in the preseason Southern Illinoisan News poll which ranked the year's prospective top teams. The list featured perennial powers from the south. Nashville, Harrisburg, Anna-Jonesboro, and Du Quoin topped the list. Thirty-five regional championships trophies filled the high school trophy cases of those four schools. Chester had yet to win a single one.

Monday, March 1, was the first day of practice. After a Saturday and Sunday of rain, the ball diamonds of Cohen Field were soaked. Kordys walked his steady frame onto the Cohen field dirt, breathing heavily into the cold 40-degree air, surveying his breath with every exhale, his feet sloshing onto the soggy infield. There was nothing auspicious about the start.

But the players were accustomed to this. Playing on a dirt infield without a tarp and in a region where it seemed as if the heavens frequently conspired against the baseball schedule, the boys were used to natural adversity. Early season practices were often held inside where the team made due with its one cage, whiffle balls, a few of Kordys's trinkets, and a little throwing practice in Colbert gym. If they were lucky enough to get outside, they got used to dealing with 40-degree days and mad March winds.

"You guys remember Hallandale?" Herb said, facing the howling wind. "Man, don't you wish we were in Florida right now?"

"Yeah," Doc agreed. "For the babes!"

Laughing, The Brothers trudged across the mushy infield and took their familiar positions.

After a quick round of catch, Kordys called for the guys to assume their positions in the field for a quick in and out in order to gauge the defensive unit. Stan Newby, former player turned assistant coach, came and stood beside Kordys who preferred an old wooden bat to hit grounders. "Man, Coach, the boys sure look smooth out there."

"They should look smooth," Kordys replied. "They've been playing together since grade school."

Unlike schools fed by many different communities, Chester High only draws from one town, Chester, and a few tiny villages on its outskirts. Since only so many athletic kids are to be found in a region of this size, the Tee Ball team looked a lot like the Khoury League team, which looked a lot like the junior high team, which looked a lot like the high school team. Kids got used to playing with each other early. If they stayed together over all those years, as The Brothers had proved, great things were possible. This year's high school team had eight members of the championship team that had won Nationals only twenty months earlier.

"Yep," said Kordys, smacking grounders that peeled out water as they skidded across the grass. "They're smooth."

Only the catching position was a question mark. Headed into this much anticipated season, Meat was a mysterious no-show on opening day. The bullish catcher who had stood his ground against The Sheriff and caught every game that Peters and Bobber threw, was absent. Almost twenty years later, Adam would attempt to explain:

"I loved ball growing up. I loved coach Kordys in junior high, but in high school our relationship began to deteriorate each year. My sophomore year I was catching in practice like I always did. I was calling balls and strikes during batting practice. I called a strike on one of the upperclass guys and he took exception and started mouthing me. I jawed back and told him he can fuck himself. At this point another upper classman started in on me. Being me, a hot head, I was like fuck you man I'll beat your ass too. This caused an end to practice and coach Kordys proceeded to chew my ass. He threw a glove at me and challenged me to fight him. He said 'Gibbs, if you think you are so tough, bring it on. I'm sick of your shit' etc. This was the turning point in our relationship. My entire junior year he was on my ass, and we got into a couple more altercations. He repeatedly told me I would never play ball for

him again, that Zach was going to be the starter next year. He treated me like I was worthless the entire year. I knew if I played for him again senior year I would end up in a knock down drag out fight. I got to the point that I started to despise the sport I had once loved. I regret to this day not playing my senior year. Looking back, I imagine coach Kordys probably thought he was trying to motivate me, and wasn't intentionally tormenting me. I was a dumb young kid with an ego and a temper. I wish I would have been more mature. That's the reason I didn't play. I couldn't see myself playing for him again." —email, Adam "Meat" Gibbs, September 26, 2014.

Meat's catcher's pads were hard to fill. Smothers Brother Zach Engel, who Kordys liked, was called upon. Known as "Z" now to his teammates, Engel had been a backup to Meat for most of his career. But now was his chance. Z was fully capable of handling the duties behind the plate. He knew his pitchers like the back of his hand and although he didn't have the raw power of Gibbs at the plate, he could hit to all fields with pop.

In left field stood the duo of Smothers Brother Matt "Herb" Seymour and Phillip Shields. Herb, standing at 5'8" and now weighing 180, was the fullback on the football team. He could bench almost 300 lbs. and was an intense competitor as he had always been, and with his blonde hair and blue eyes, had confidence in talking to the pretty girls. After a year of dating a cute, blonde freshman, The Brothers started referring to him as "Ken," and his girlfriend, Barbie.

Shields, a lifelong fan of the game, worshipped the

St. Louis Cardinals. Phil was undersized and overmatched for the high school game. He knew it but didn't give a lick, happy just to be there in the open field, the bats cracking, the leather popping—even at 40 degrees.

In center, standing next to Junior Phil Grau, a 5'7", sturdy, speedy, left-handed outfielder and pitcher, was Brandon "Bundy" Brown. Bundy, one of the four seniors on the team, possessed an excellent arm, hit for power, and could run down almost anything hit into the outfield grass.

About fifty feet to the left of the centerfielders in right field, stood Bobber and sophomore Derek Link. Derek, a lefthanded pitcher/outfielder was slotted to be one of the four pitchers the Jackets would be using this season and would potentially see some time in the outfield.

Bobber, now 6'2" and weighing 185 lbs., was slowly and imperceptibly to himself becoming the athlete he always dreamed of being. Although his bum leg was still giving him problems, he was feeling strong. He had grown into a patient, sweet swinging, all-around hitter, a fast and smooth, long stride outfielder, a crafty, Picasso of a pitcher, and perhaps the most driven kid on the team.

Taking ground balls at third was senior Little Bruce "Poop" Luthy, and sophomore, Eric Caby. Little wasn't a term describing Bruce's physique. Standing at 5'10" tall and weighing 230 lbs., he was anything but. After a childhood of baseball that entailed fielding endless grounds balls from his father, Poop was a sure-handed fielder who carried a big stick at the plate. Poop was the nickname "Little Bruce" had been tagged with during basketball season when he checked into a game after a quick trip to the john, a stream of toilet paper clinging to his leg. The nickname stuck with him over the years. His backup was sophomore Eric Caby, another strong football player type who could also hit the ball a very long way if given the chance.

Next to them at shortstop was Jarrod Peters. Peters still had the scowl of an outlaw and a meanness that he seemed to bring with him to the ballpark. Junior Jeremy Blechle was Peters's backup. Peters, the quarterback on the football team and one of the team's captains, had obvious abilities. He had the strongest arm on the team, hit for the most power, and arguably possessed the surest glove in the infield. "He could hit the ball a country mile," quipped a *Chester Herald* reporter the previous year. Peters had developed into not only one of the team's best players but also its indisputable leader. The boys looked up to his meanness. Kordys would try to call his pitches. Peters would shake him off.

At the Keystone Sack, second base, was the last senior on the team, Michael Knop. Knop had been a solid, steady player ever since his years in Khoury League. He had a set of great hands, rarely made errors, and was well versed in turning the double play. First base was a position up for grabs. Doc and junior reserve Brad Butler split the reps on this day. Penciling in a starter was going to be a difficult decision. All the boys could field and catch. Batting, however, required some measure of skill beyond courage—but it began with courage. "We'll see," Kordys said.

Of course, if the team wanted honor and notoriety, they needed to play well. After nearly a month of bouncing back and forth between the field and the gym, the boys opened their season against cross-county rival, Steeleville, a town of 2,000 just thirteen miles east of Chester. Thirteen miles in Illinois country was a long way in some sense, though only 13 minutes or less away as the truck flies. Each little town seen from afar on the prairie with its maple trees huddling around a church steeple and a water tower, the only thing taller than the church, advertising with no sense of pretension the name of the town—Nashville, Steelville, or, more quaintly, Red Bud—had its own personality. Sometimes you just didn't like the neighboring town. If they ever beat you in sports, you might not show your face there for a year, out of humiliation.

On game day, Kordys usually arrived at the field close to the same time the players did. As he made his way up the sidewalk to Cohen Field on opening day, he spied a group of players in the outfield grass playing a game of pepper while another group stood by observing. Stepping foot across the threshold of the third base dugout, he was met by another familiar face. "Cccoach, I can do the book today," stuttered a husky seventeen-year-old wearing glasses and a Chester football hoodie. Kordys smiled. Eric Skorcz was a longtime favorite of Kordys and as close to a mascot as the team had. A high school sports fanatic, Eric was a lineman on the football team, attended every basketball game, and grew up playing Khoury league with some of the guys. He was a hard worker, well respected, and friends with all.

As Kordys jotted down his team's opening day lineup, Skorcz laid out the team's five beat-up navy blue batting helmets, a bucket of throwing balls, and the three team bats. The bats were hung up in a row. First, was the orange and black 33″ 28 oz. C-Core Model, second, a 33″, 28 oz. Scandium Easton Redline, and last, a 36″-34 oz. Easton Black Magic Model 1990.

The C-Core and Redline were sacred. If ever a legal bat was produced that performed like an illegal one, it was these bats. "Th*hh*eese are the best aluminum bats ever," Skorcz said proudly, as he sat on the cold metal bench.

But Kordy's knew it wasn't about the bat, but the boy swinging it.

The Black Magic was a different matter. Over-sized, solid, character-filled, it was a memento from Jacket teams of the past, and served as a reminder of the identity of the team, a hard-working, blue-collar team. "Eric," said Peters, as he kicked dirt off his cleats, "make sure that bat gets taken to every game this year." He meant the Black Magic. "That bat is lucky."

Kordys handed Skorcz the scorebook and lineup card asking him to copy the line-up into the book. The Jacket lineup looked like this:

1.#32 Brandon "Bundy" Brown CF
2.#24 Phil Grau RF
3.#16 Jarrod Peters P
4.#20 Bruce "Poop" Luthy 3B
5.#12 Bobber 1B
6.#22 Zach "Z" Engel C
7.#10 Michael Knop 2B
8.#14 Matt "Herb" Seymour LF
9.#28 Jeremy Blechle SS
Subs: #17 Matt "Doc" Davitz (Note: 1b if Bobber pitches), #21 Jake Arbeiter, #31 Brad Butler, #7 Phil Shields, #13 Derek Link, #30 Eric Caby, #35 Josh Hecht
Coaches: Jeff Kordys, Stan Newby, Jeremy Williamson

On this day, the usual challenges of playing early spring baseball were all present. The windbreaker temperature and the wind, the wet field, water seeping up at every puncture of the cleats—with these conditions, only the "regulars" would be showing up to watch on this day. There would be the Ohlaus, The Warden, Big Luthy, and the other parents. Bobber's grandpa with the sciatica would have to stay in his car, but he would honk whenever Bobber came to the plate and honk more when Bobber got a hit. Big Luthy would be sitting tense in the front row or pacing the sideline. He wouldn't even blink once a ball was on its way. Kordys counted only about twenty fans scattered in the bleachers and lawn chairs down the third base fence line. The boys didn't even glance up to see the most dependable persons in their life. They knew they were there. Twenty of them.

It was enough.

The Jackets wasted no time. They had been waiting for this moment for three pewter gray months of winter. After Peters struck out the side in the top half of the first on hissing fastballs limning the edges, Bundy Brown singled, stole a base, and was knocked in immediately by Grau.

The Jackets would add another run the following inning, a leadoff double by Bobber was followed by a Knop single. In the bottom of the sixth, Luthy walked to lead off the inning. "Good eye!" his father approved (though he would have much preferred a triple down the third base line). Bobber, a hungry expression still on his face, hit another double. Grampa honked twice. Then Z doubled in Bobber to make it 4–1.

Though Chester seemed to have all earthly elements under control, in the top of the seventh a brutal lightning storm came creeping into the landscape. Distant flashes seemed like alien strikes meant to take out small-town water towers and strike at steeples. Only four dads remained in the stands, Danny Ohlau, Big Bruce, The Warden, and one monumental figure near the dugout, The Sheriff. The winds picked up, and routine fly balls became impossible to track. Steeleville showed something of their eponymous heritage. They weren't about to give up. In the last inning, they cut the

Jacket lead to 4–3, runners on first and second with one out. On his 118th pitch, Peters induced a game-winning 6-4-3 double play. Bobber at first base kept the final out in his glove as the Yellow Jackets raced off the cold soppy Cohen field grounds with a hard-fought 4–3 victory over their county rival.

The boys scampered to their cars through an assault of icy rain. Eric, game summaries flapping in the wind, wasn't far behind. "Freddy, I can't believe we got this game in," said Kordys to The Sheriff. He screwed his manager's cap on tight and made for the car.

Before the boys dispersed into the terrible night, some fretted about their errors. They had Steeleville on the ropes then let them back in the game. The boys knew if they were going to reach their goals, a much better performance, something nearing perfection, was required of them.

But back at Cohen Field, the last to leave, one man knew what he had just seen. "Damn," The Sheriff said to himself, shaking his head in the rain. "That's the best damn team this county has ever seen." Save for one missing piece. Where was Meat?

CHAPTER FIFTEEN
Interrupted Play

*There's the story of a young radio broadcaster in the 1930s,
fresh out of college, who was broadcasting the Chicago Cubs
games from a tiny Iowa radio station, relayed via telegraph.
During one game, telegraph communication was interrupted.
The inventive young broadcaster had McGee fouling off pitch
after pitch. When transmission was reconnected, McGee was
on third. The broadcaster's name was Ronald Reagan.*

Chester's schedule called for back to back to back
games to start the season. Kordys liked it this way
because he knew his club was saturated with the good
pitching needed to string together wins. With Peters at
the top, Bobber behind him, and Phil Grau and Derek
Link at three and four, the staff was loaded for firing.

The storm of the previous night dampened the plans
for an away game twenty-three miles north in the town
of Red Bud. Red Bud called Chester to report on the
state of their ball diamond. They'd need another day, the
spring winds whipping across the farmland would dry
it out soon. They'd have to cancel. The cancellation was
agonizing for the boys of Chester. They felt their engines
just warming up. They wanted to play.

Most of the players had long forgotten their faults

from the opening game, but not Bobber. Despite his talents, he remained driven by an odd sense of inferiority. Growing up behind his older brother, Bobber always felt like he had to prove something to somebody. Nothing ever seemed good enough for him. Two for three with two doubles was not enough; 40 points on the basketball court wasn't enough; 16:00 in the three-mile wasn't fast enough. He needed to do more, and he didn't want to wait until the next game to try.

A day later, Marissa came to town. Another small town of around 2,000, the Marissa Meteors brought with them a storied baseball history which included a State Championship from the 1986 season and, as memory served some of the residents, the hometown of the great Warren Hacker of the Chicago Cubs who in 1952 had been 23rd in voting for MVP. "Twenny-t'ird," said the old German residents of Marissa. "Dat ain't bad."

The Jackets didn't care about the history of the Meteors so much as the presence. All they cared about was getting their team on track and winning the game. Bobber would be handling the duties on the mound.

There were no excuses on this day for the bad defense. The Jacket fielders committed eight errors behind their lefty hurler. Although abundant, the mistakes didn't break the back of the home team. Behind a five-hit complete game by their pitcher and a 3-for-4 day at the plate with a home run and four RBI's from Luthy, Chester survived with a 6–5 victory moving them to 2–0 on the infant season.

. . . . .

Waterloo

The following week saw more of the same for the Chester defense. After a thrashing of Shawnee High School on Monday, the boys and Kordys prepared for the 40-minute drive north to Gibault High School, a Catholic school in the town of Waterloo.

Released from class an hour early, the boys hurried through the gymnasium, down the steps leading to the gym floor, dashed under the scoreboard, through the tunnel, and into the varsity locker room. The locker room was built in the 1920s. Its lockers banged shut with the same sound your grandfather and father heard.

It contained three long rows of orange lockers, two long varnished wooden benches in the middle of the room, a communal shower, two sinks, a chipped urinal, and a toilet. It was spacious compared to how some of the boys experienced it during football.

Pulling on their white pin-stripes with the cartoonish bumblebee logo over the heart, the boys made their way to the long, yellow bus idling in the parking lot. Behind the wheel was Omer Knop, grandfather to second baseman Michael. Beaming from ear to ear, he would greet each player with a "Go get 'em today" or a "Let's bring home a win" as the players one by one hopped up the two steps onto his bus.

"Should be an easy one today," Peters told Omer and patted him confidently on the shoulder.

It should have been. The Yellow Jackets outmatched the Hawks from Gibault at almost every position. It didn't matter. Although the boys from Chester outhit the Hawks twelve to eight, Chester was once again sloppy in the field, making nine errors. The miscues allowed the inferior team to score thirteen runs to the Yellow Jackets' twelve. It was the first, stinging, loss of the short season.

The bus ride home was poignantly opposite the ride home from Shawnee, a week earlier, when the boys dropped the bus windows wide to let out the Beach Boys all the way up Route 3. Like many rides home after a loss, this one was quiet as a funeral home. The seating arrangement on the bus saw the boys separated into cliques. The quiet, walk man listeners were positioned near the front, the seniors in the back, and The Brothers usually congregated in the middle.

As the bus was entering Ellis Grove, ten miles from the high school, a quiet ride was suddenly interrupted by a small commotion and laughter coming from the last two seats.

"What's going on back there?" whispered Shields to Engel as he saw Doc and Bobber standing up in the aisle.

Z craned his neck to see. "They must be messing around with Herb in the back."

Kordys seemed immune to the issue as he sat in the front, busily adding up the day's stat line from the book, still fuming from the loss and the unfathomable number of errors.

Herb was sleeping in the back. With Herb wheezing

asthmatically in the last seat, Jarrod concocted a plan. "Give me that fishing line from my bag."

Managing to slip Herb's hat off his head, fishing twine (leftover from bass fishing Little Mary's creek the weekend before) in hand, Peters knotted the twine through the small holes in the top of the hat and cast it out the window. With over sixty feet of line, he had more than enough to trail it behind the bus. "We may even get some cars to run over it," he snickered to Luthy.

There it was, Herb's orange and black, flex fitted, Yellow Jacket cap dragging on the asphalt fitted road, bouncing in the red glow of the bus's tail lights. It was not known how the "Yellow Jackets" had come to have orange on their uniforms, but now the orange looked comically appropriate bouncing on the highway behind the bus. Releasing more and more twine, the boys let the hat make its way farther and farther away from the rear of the bus, until it nearly slid under a following car. Quiet commotion quickly turned into loud commotion. "Sit down back there!" yelled Kordys. "And get your hands and anything outside that window inside the bus!" He was still mad about the game. Had they won, he would have let them dangle freshmen out the window by their ankles, for all that.

The seniors in the back of the bus slunk down and laughed into their fists. After reeling in Herb's cap, which now looked like the material equivalent of road kill, Peters gently placed it back on the head of the sleeping junior.

"Now what hat am I going to wear?" Herb said,

puzzled and pissed off and trying to wake up from the nightmare. "Jarrod, why are you such a dick?"

By the time Herb was fully awake and cooled down, Omer had the big yellow bus nestled up to the back of Colbert Gymnasium. Kordys, always straightforward, kept his remarks simple as his team exited the bus. "Game tomorrow versus Trico at home. Can't make nine errors if we want to win."

As Bobber exited the bus on that cold spring night, he vowed *never again lose to a team like that*. Then he stopped and reset. *Never again to lose.*

CHAPTER SIXTEEN
ACT

By the end of the third week of the season, Chester had bounced back from the early loss in Waterloo. They were 6–1 now, reaping the benefits of improved glove work in the field. The defense had secured the team wins versus county rivals Sparta and Trico, as well as Dupo. Now the boys prepped for their first weekend set of the young season, The Ste. Genevieve tournament.

The tournament itself did not appear like it was going to be much of a test for the rallying Jackets. Ste. Genevieve and Granville High Schools from Missouri didn't bring with them the baseball clout of southern Illinois powers Nashville, Harrisburg, and Du Quoin of the River to River Conference. The two-game tourney would be an easy test for the student athletes of Chester—much easier than the test that preceded it that day.

The ACT is an inscrutable obstacle devised by evil men that tests the college bound innocent on the R's of Reading, Writing, and Arithmetic—then throws in Science as a cruel joke—in the hopes of securing the student's failure and preventing him from ever playing college sports. In other words, it's a fair test.

But the baseball players of Chester didn't think so. This year, the spring exam date just so happened to be April 10, the same date as the tournament.

There was nothing the boys loved more than playing the game of baseball. They couldn't believe they were going to have to miss a baseball game for this ACT test.

"It is not some ridiculous test," Sharon told her son the morning of Saturday, April 10, 1999. "This test could determine where you end up going to college or how much in scholarships you may receive."

That spiel may have worked for some, but not for Bobber. He wasn't the type to make taking the ACT a higher priority than playing baseball. "It's a flawed test anyway," he told his mom, as though he had researched the matter deeply. "How is a college supposed to tell how smart or stupid a kid is by one test? Besides," he added inarguably, "we have a game."

The Jackets had a doubleheader in Missouri, and five of the players, all juniors, would have to take the test: Bobber, Phil Grau, Doc, Engel, and Jake Arbeiter. Kordys had planned for the five to completely miss the first game against the Dragons scheduled for 11:00 a.m. and be late for the 1:30 p.m. game versus Glanville.

At 7:15 a.m., the rumbling of Phil's '88 Camaro at Light and Swanwick let Bobber know that it was time to submit to the requirements of virtually every college in the country with a baseball team. Doc was already in the car. Phil peeled out toward the test site. The prospect of missing the doubleheader was compounding their nervousness about this four-hour standardized exam—

and vice versa.

"You think we're going to be able to make it before the start of the second game?" Bobber said to Doc.

"You're asking the wrong guy. Ask the guy behind the wheel." Doc looked at Phil.

"What is it, like an hour to Ste. Gen?" Phil asked. Then he answered with a promising rev. "Cam can."

As the boys reached the library at Sparta High School, the location where they would be taking the test, they were assigned seats relatively close to one another.

The test itself was brutal, just as advertised. All the years of throwing spitballs in class and dreaming out the classroom window were coming back to haunt The Brothers. Their Chester education had little prepared them for the inscrutable questions of the test, with its version of English, Math, Reading, and Science. After over three hours of filling in ovals, Bobber felt like snapping his No. 2 pencil in half. Surreptitiously glancing two rows over at Doc, then shooting Phil a quick look, he noticed his buddies were finished as well. The trio had completed the test, but there was no leaving early. The ACT proctors were notoriously evil. Once they had disqualified a kid for sniffing.

Each test taker had to wait the allotted time in order for everyone to leave. The clock read 11:18 p.m. "Can't we just leave?" Bobber mouthed to Doc. "I'm walking out."

Twelve minutes seemed like an eternity. "Okay, put your pencils down," said the evil proctor, who otherwise looked like a nice fourth-grade teacher.

"Congratulations, you have now completed the ACT, close your booklets and gather your belongings."

"Let's get the hell out of here," The Brothers agreed as though their kidnapper had just opened a window.

As they ran down the hall, it felt like Mr. Lochead was going to yell at them from behind but they burst out the doors and could see Phil's red Camaro shining in the midday sun.

"Shotgun," called Bobber.

"Cam can!" they hollered and peeled out of the Sparta parking lot.

After their quick stop at Taco Barn, burritos in hand, Phil stepped on the gas, and they were off again. Somewhere in Missouri, their buddies were trying to buy time by fouling off pitches. The Brothers were on their way. Taco lettuce flew out the window and shreds of cheese smeared into Phil's duct taped upholstery. With the first warm day of spring upon them, and the biggest academic test of their lives behind them, they rambled down Route 150, letting the fresh breeze shoot through the open T-top of the car. Bad Company's "Shooting Star" throbbed from Cam's speakers.

The clock read twelve noon. The muscle car needed to travel the 53 miles to reach Ste Gen. in less than an hour, the three figured, not as tired as they thought at doing story problems. Cam can.

Cam rushed its way through Chester and over the bridge, its average speed about seventy miles per hour. That number was sure to increase as the group made their way to the Missouri side of the river, where the flat, straight roads of the river's flood plain laid a smooth track to Saint Genevieve.

"It's only taken us twenty-nine minutes to St. Mary," Doc reported, studying his ACT watch and calculator with a now very practical interest. St. Mary was a small village of 360, nestled up to an offshoot of the Mississippi River that separated it from Kaskaskia Island. "We're only ten miles away from Saint Gen."

To the population sign of St. Mary, Phil's heavy foot had been more out of necessity than pleasure. Now, knowing that they were good on time, the boys relaxed. They had missed Game 1, but would make it in plenty of time for Game 2. Sitting back and letting the last of the burrito wrappers escape out the window in careless wads, the boys could now enjoy Phil's car for the purpose he had bought it.

Bobber looked to the back seat where Doc was putting his Hewlett-Packard back in its case. They nodded.

"What's this got under the hood?" Bobber asked Phil, and then, almost on cue the three said, "Cam can."

As the road out of town straightened, Phil put the pedal to the floor, the speedometer ascended to 110 mph.

"I'm glad Joni ain't drivin'!" Bobber called into the wind.

Squatting on a side road was what looked to be a police car. "You have got to be kidding me," said Phil as his Camaro sped past the would-be cop car. "I'm not slowing down. If he wants to give me a ticket, he's going to have to catch me."

"If he catches us," yelled Doc, leaning forward into the wind, "tell him we just took the ACT and can't think anymore." It wasn't far from the truth. "I'm sure he'll understand."

If it was a cop, he wasn't in the mood for a chase. Probably enjoying a doughnut and some dunking coffee. On the fumes of adrenaline, Phil and the boys sped down Highway 61, nervously looking back to see if there were any pretty lights in their rear view.

When they skid to a stop at the tournament site, Kordy's greeted them. "'Bout time you got here. We won the first game."

CHAPTER SEVENTEEN
Getting Noticed

On Monday, the players gathered in their usual spot in the library on the third floor of the main building at CHS. They pored studiously over the most important literature in the school library whose genre they had mastered: the sports section of *The Chester Herald Tribune* and the *Southern Illinoisan*. There were four copies of each, and the boys almost literally tore into them.

"CHS Baseball Wins Ste. Genevieve Tournament, Now 8–1," the headline of the *Herald* heralded. "This year's team is good, very good," it went on to say. The boys ogled the words and read more carefully than they had *The Great Gatsby* how great the Jackets had performed over the weekend.

Sifting through the pages of the *Southern Illinoisan*, Doc came across something that caught his eye. "Hey, Bobber, take a look at this."

Jim Gordillo, baseball writer for the *Southern*, covered nearly one hundred schools, from Mount Vernon in the northern part of his region all the way down to Cairo and Massac County at the southern apex of the state. He knew pretty much every highway and backroad in southern Illinois and knew his high school sports history when it came to baseball. He knew that Chester had only one conference crown in its trophy case. From 1976. He wasn't about to rank the boys in orange and black above the other perennial powers in the South until they had proven something.

"He has us ranked seventh," Doc frowned.

"Seventh?" they puzzled and began muttering.

"We should be number one," said Bobber angrily.

But to get the respect of a veteran sportswriter and top the rankings, they all knew what had to be done. They needed to do more than beat the small schools on the docket. They needed to win the conference and to do so meant beating the teams ranked higher than them in the poll.

The next three weeks saw Chester collect many of those types of wins. The Yellow Jackets thumped Ste. Genevieve 14–0, rolled past Anna-Jonesboro 11–2, beat rival Du Quoin 8–5, handled non-conference foe New Athens 8–2, edged out A-J at home 3–1, and collected wins versus Steeleville, Trico, Sparta, and two from Pinkneyville. With wins piling up, the Jackets were getting noticed. Bobber was hitting .539, Luthy .490, Peters was 6–0 on the mound with five home runs at the plate, and their record stood at 17–2. Only one loss during that stretch further marred their record, a loss to arch-rival Nashville.

The drubbing came at the hands of Zach Borowiak, Nashville's star shortstop and pitcher and one of southern Illinois' best hitters, who three years later would get drafted and spend half his minor league career in Triple-A with the Red Sox. Everyone knew Borowiak, the mention of whose name now sat in Bobber's stomach like an acid.

During the game Nashville had pounded the lefty pitcher, roughing him up for twelve runs and twelve hits in five innings of work, giving him his only loss of the season. It was something Chester hadn't seen, a team that could hit as well as they could, with good pitching to match.

The Jackets were going to get their shot at revenge, however, as Nashville was slotted to come to town on Friday, May 7. If they were going to beat the feared Hornets and claim top spot in the Mississippi Division of the River to River, they would to have to match Nashville in every facet of the game.

The Nashville-Chester game came on a cool and windy Friday at the Cohen Complex. The Hornets of Nashville versus the Yellow Jackets of Chester, two teams named for the only feared creatures the prairies of Illinois had not been cleared of. The Hornets, coming in as the favorites, already had twenty wins under their belts—but now they were coming to Chester's field.

Just as in basketball there is such a thing as a homecourt advantage, the familiarity of the setting, the depth perception, the tension on the rims, the sound of the hard maple, so too in baseball there is home field advantage that is something quite apart from three generations of family and your best girl in the stands. Kordys was starting to wonder whether that eight error game against Steeleville wasn't the result of an unfamiliar field. But as he watched his team scoop grounders off the cool dirt of Cohen, he sensed an advantage. Every farm boy knows his dirt.

Danny Ohlau was there, straight from work, joining The Warden, Big Luthy and The Sheriff along the fence, and Sharon with the other moms in lawn chairs, wrapped in wool shawls. Grampa Ohlau sat ready to toot his horn from the parking lot. Big Bruce paced the fence line. As the game began, frost formed on the fence.

Chester came out of the gates like a team set on retribution. Nothing settles the nerves like revenge. If they won, they all knew, they would put themselves in the driver's seat for their first ever S.I.R.R. baseball conference championship.

Z started off the scoring, jacking a Brock Holston offering over the left field fence, scoring Luthy and Bobber in the bottom of the second. Sharon Ohlau clapped loud beneath the shawl.

As expected, Peters came out sharp and mean, working his fastball and slider on the outer half, scattering two hits in the first two innings and striking out the side in the third.

Nashville, with a pair of seeing-eye base hits in the fourth, scored two runs, tightening things, 3–2, before Chester could make it up to bat in the bottom of the inning. Then in stepped Bundy Brown.

Bundy, not nearly as cocky as some of the other stars on the team—the *Herald* rarely mentioned him—was just as steady, sure-handed as a mechanic and reliable as a farmhand. After the season was over, Kordys reflected, giving Bundy his due as "the best leadoff guy who could hit for power and average and a center fielder who could make any play, probably one of the best outfielders in the state that season."

When Bundy came up and sparked the fourth inning rally, it was no surprise to The Brothers and the coach. He jumped on a fastball early in the count and was able to lift a leadoff home run deep to left-center, sparking a four-run fourth. Now Chester led 7–2.

The next inning, Chester threatened again, loading the bases, but failed to score. The Hornets began gathering a little momentum. Peters was tiring noticeably. In the top of the sixth, Nashville loaded the bases with only one out. Two hits and a sacrifice fly later, and the score was 7–5. Big Bruce's pace hastened on the fence line. Sharon tightened the shawl around her shoulders. Danny Ohlau, stoic and unmoved, sent out a simple reminder: "You can do it, boys."

With a narrow two-run lead in the seventh, Peters allowed the first two men to reach base. A couple of sacrifice bunts and a gracious call by the home plate ump and the game was tied, 7–7.

Extra innings. Phil Grau, took over pitching duties from Peters who cursed himself audibly. Grau walked the first batter, his arm still warming up, but lured the second into swinging at a curve in the dirt for a strikeout. A fly ball to Bundy in center followed for out number two, and the Hornet's fourth batter was only able to manage a weak come backer for the third out of the inning. This set up the Chester eighth.

As the Chester batters grabbed the cold handles of the bats, they looked out to the mound. Borowiak.

Zach Borowiak had been put in to hold down the Jackets the rest of the way. He quickly sent the first two Chester batters back to the dugout. But then came Bundy to the plate. Chester's fire starter once again stepped to the plate and seemed to have no fear of Borowiak. Rising to their feet, the Chester bench knew if Bundy were to get on base, Peters, Luthy, and Bobber would follow. Peters on deck, stopped cursing himself and screamed at Bundy and alternately heckling Borowiak. There is no high school sport short of debate where communication is more a weapon. In basketball, of course, the home crowd goes insane as the opposing guard tries to sink a one-and-one free throw with no time remaining. In track and cross country there is no eloquence in the single one syllable word "Go!" You could just imagine a golfer—no true Chester sportsman would touch a sissy golf club until his knees prevented him from playing a true sport—trying to sink a putt on the 18th Hole with the crowd jeering. But in baseball, there is time for narrative. Personal accounts are to be expected. A girlfriend's name was not off limits, though one's mother was. Mispronouncing of names is one form of acceptable defamation.

"Booooar-yak!" the Chester bench defamed. They wanted to let the future Major Leaguer know that he was still in Chester.

"Let's go, Bundy!" Peters demanded, the veins popping in his neck.

"All we need is a base runner," Kordys agreed.

Whether it was the weather or the pressure, or the comment about his girlfriend, the Nashville star threw four straight balls. Chester's leadoff man was on first.

Kordys didn't wait long to make a move. He went directly to his right cheek for the indicator, then after some gestures as traditional as those of the Catholic priest at Saint Mary's, he runs his hand across his chest. Bundy was to steal.

Lifting his strong leg, unsuspecting of the theft attempt, Borowiak fired home. The ball whizzed past Borowiak, and Bundy dove in just ahead of the throw. "Safe!" barked the ump. The Chester bench went ballistic. Revenge was one hit away.

At the plate stood Chester's home run leader, and with two outs in a tie game and a runner on second, it was an easy decision for the experienced coach from Nashville. He signaled to the home plate umpire that he was intentionally putting Peters on first. Peters, disgusted, walked down to first, glaring at Borowiak. "Fuckin' chicken."

Borowiak was more bull than chicken. He would have loved to strike Peters out. But the Nashville coach, wisely no doubt, opted for Luthy. There was just one flaw in the plan.

Luthy knew how to take a pitch better than anyone on the team. Borowiak, continued to struggle with the strike zone and walked him on five pitches.

Up to the plate came Bobber.

All season Bobber had been one of Chester's best

producers, leading the team in hits and runs batted in. He was well accustomed to cleaning up the occasional mess left behind by Peters or Luthy, the former sometimes too eager the latter sometimes too patient. Now was his chance to wreak revenge on the team that had embarrassed him two weeks earlier.

With the cold wind howling from the northwest, blowing swiftly across the field from left to right, Bobber stepped in and then out of the batter's box. He was toying with Borowiak. "Let him think about it," Bobber told himself.

"He's gotta come to you," he heard his dad say, but he wasn't sure whether it was in his head he heard it or from the other side of the fence. He knew Grampa would be ready to toot and that his mom would be cuddling herself in her shawl and doing the one thing that was in the end more important than an entire childhood of preparation. She would be praying.

Bobber dug into the cold dirt of the box. Two outs, bases loaded, tie game—Borowiak had to come after him. *If it's in the zone*, Bobber coached himself, *I'm swingin' at the first pitch.*

Borowiak was getting cold. He blew into his pitching hand. Bobber stepped out of the box one more time, patiently wrenching his bat. He stepped in. The first pitch from Borowiak came at about the same speed that Phil had driven to Ste. Genevieve. Eighty-four miles per hour, The Sheriff's radar gun read. Waiting for it to reach him, with his smooth, controlled swing, Bobber made perfect contact with the ball. Freezing at third,

Bundy stood, making sure the ball cleared the third baseman. Flying directly over the third baseman's head, the ball reached the outfield grass. Sprinting over to make the play was Nashville's left fielder. By the time the line drive reached him, the brisk wind had already knocked it down. Racing home, Bundy was greeted by the ecstatic on-deck hitter, Michael Knop and joined by a stampede.

The Yellow Jackets celebrated the victory at home plate hugging and high fiving and smacking Bobber and Bundy on the head and shoulders as the Hornets despondently walked off the field. Standing up now from the cold metal bleachers, the bundled up orange and black diehards clapped and cheered for their beloved Jackets.

"Great job, men," Kordys told them in the huddle after the game. "I know you are all excited. I'm excited too, but there is still work to be done. We have Du Quoin on Tuesday which could determine conference or not. Let's enjoy the win for the next hour or so, and then refocus our minds to the next game."

For the next hour *or so*. A high schooler's life was pretty much demarcated in hours. First hour class, fifth hour study hall, 4 pm practice.

"Make that one hour to enjoy it," Kordys said. "Everybody here agree that one hour from now, you'll start focusing on Du Quoin."

Still ranked second in Southern Illinois, two spots ahead of Chester, Du Quoin had several college signees. They had no known weaknesses. But the Du Quoin, seen from the vantage of a year's maturity, had one thing against them: they were the team that had dramatically eliminated the Jackets from state contention the year before.

"Revenge," said Bobber, before the hour was up.

. . . . .

Two days passed, the Jackets impatiently waiting for the Indians to come to town. Du Quoin was relying on ace Nolan Bastien, a big, powerful, intimidating presence and a recent Rend Lake College signee, to spoil the Chester hopes of making school history. The Jacket players, however, weren't in the least bit intimidated. This outing proved to be the fourth time in two years that most of Kordys' players would be seeing the big ace from Du Quoin.

Familiarity helped Chester. With big first and third innings and shaky Indian defense, the Jackets catapulted to a 5–0 lead. Solid Jacket defense and a five-hitter from Bobber secured a 5–2 win. Chester now wore the conference crown.

Winning the conference was impressive for a school like Chester, but the feat wasn't even close to what they ultimately wanted to accomplish. Their goal was simple. It had always been to make it to Lanphier Park in Springfield, the state capital of Illinois, and win it all— the State Championship.

CHAPTER EIGHTEEN
Veni, Vidi, Vici

Love of Baseball

Baseball is a lot about feeling and waiting to feel. Feeling the sharp metal cleats that the great and cruel Ty Cobb once cleaned threateningly on his opponent's dugout steps pierce the hot summer dust of the ball diamond ... waiting the hundredth time, your fist punching into the leather pocket, for the next ground ball or pop up ... studying, imagining, in the on-deck circle, waiting for the chance to lift the team, feel the thrill, all eyes in attendance watching you in awe, the Little Leaguers clinging to the fence as though it were magnetic ... the smell of the chalk and the dirt and the leather, the pose of the stance, the pure feeling from palm to shoulder of solid connection and the euphoric rise in emotion as your young legs carry you around the bases ... diving into third after a leadoff triple, tearing the skin off your leg and bouncing up and dusting off the dirt that it would take your mom two wash cycles to get out.

Is there any other moment in life other than death and farming where you feel so close to the earth?

For the people of Chester, any success at all in baseball was success enough. For years, the football team, pride of the town, played second fiddle to conference rival Du Quoin, while the basketball team, unable to win a regional since its first and only one in 1975, struggled to have even a winning season. High school baseball in Chester was starved for success, and for the boys to bring home the school's first ever S.I.R.R. Championship at the expense of rivals Nashville and Du Quoin meant something.

"We're so proud of you," they heard from every mom and dad on the team.

Of course, the boys saw it differently. Every game now was an elimination game—lose, and the season would end. For the seniors, their high school baseball careers would end. None of the parents discussed how they were only three wins from Sectionals—only five wins from State. For the boys, especially for The Brothers, this was about doing what they had always dreamed of doing. It was about creating their legacy, the kind that never dies in a town as small and as close knit as Chester.

The "Regional Preview" in the Southern Illinoisan made for as good a read at the Main Street Tap as it did in fifth-hour study hall:

"If Chester had a trophy case specifically for the baseball program, it would be very small, and very empty," wrote Gordillo. "A lone district championship from 1949 is the pride of the Yellow Jacket program. But that could change this year. Chester is 23–2, one of the best seasons ever in school history." Then Gordillo summed up the drama: "One problem, defending regional champ Du Quoin stands in the way." But he added prophetically, that Chester had 39 homers on the season. "And with the regional at Du Quoin, the Indians' small park plays right into the Yellow Jackets' hands."

Finally, Gordillo was on their side. The boys in fifth-hour study hall sat back with the first feeling of smugness all season — all except Bobber that is.

"He didn't say nothin' about State."

The boys looked at Bobber, the least likely to cry after a defeat, the most likely to make a big play for a win.

"That'll be in next week's paper," Doc chimed in.

Chester (23–2), a school without a regional championship to its name, was trying to change the course of its own history, a task which for a river town seemed — well, like changing the course of the river. Du Quoin (19–11), with almost twenty wins of its own was the second seed and a damnable foe. A couple of teams capable of the upset were No. 3 Trico (13–7), a team with strong pitching, and No. 4 Steeleville (11–7) who had nearly beaten the Jackets early in the season.

A year after their heartbreak defeat at the hands of Du Quoin, the Jackets found themselves in familiar territory. After wins over small schools like Ziegler-Royalton-Christopher and Waltonville High School, Chester was once again in the regional final. But who would they play?

"Trico upsets Indians," the *Southern* headline read the morning of May 23, the last day of the school year in

Chester. Danny, who was eating Cheerios and getting ready for a Friday morning at the prison, motioned to his son who was sitting next to him, working on his second bowl. "You should read this," he said pointing to the article. "Looks like you guys play Trico tomorrow. Jeremy and Josh [Kranawetter] had good games. They beat Du Quoin 16–8."

"That's good for us," a surprised Bobber replied. "I'd much rather face them anyway."

Although the Jackets had beaten the Pioneers twice already, each game proved a dogfight. Trico's head coach, Gary Glidewell, knew that his team stood a good chance of upsetting the favored Jackets, especially with hard-throwing ace Josh Kranawetter set to take the mound. Glidewell didn't seem overly impressed with the hard-hitting Chester offense. "The first time, we should have beaten Chester for sure," Glidewell told Gordillo. "The second time, if we make a few plays we could have beaten them. We know they are good, but we feel like we are just as good."

The Pioneer players were easy to spot on Saturday afternoon at Indian Field, site of the regional finals. They came wearing their royal blue, yellow trimmed Pioneer jerseys and hats. The pioneer fans, wearing the same colors, set up lawn chairs, lining the first base line, getting set for what could end up being their school's first regional crown since 1973.

"Play ball!" yelled the ump, and there was a new energy in the crack of applause from both sides.

Peters, on the hill, peered in at Z after the Jackets

failed to push anyone across in the top half of the inning, focusing on one thing: starting strong. All season he had used his eighty-five mile per hour fastball and sharp curve to stymie hitters. His father, The Sheriff, who had been at every one of his son's games since Tee-ball, always told him, "Son, you have a great arm. Use it. Challenge every hitter. Never fear anyone."

Chester opened up scoring in the top of the third when Grau laced an RBI single through the hole at third. 1–0 Chester. Jeremy Kranawetter would come back in the bottom of the inning with a single of his own to tie it at 1–1. It wouldn't stay tied for long.

"They came, they saw, and they conquered," boasted the *Herald*, perhaps sensing as much as creating a mini-southern Illinois high school epic. Chester's offensive onslaught was historic. "It was a straight fastball that ran down and in," Bobber had told the reporter, describing the Kranawetter pitch in the fourth. "All I did was drop the bat head, and with the short porch in right, the ball went over it."

It was a modest self-assessment, and Bobber read his own words in the newspaper with satisfaction. Bobber's two-run blast preceded a three-run bomb by Bundy, which gave the Yellow Jackets a commanding 6–1 lead. After the fourth inning barrage, Chester added two more runs in the fifth, and three more in the seventh. Peters made absolute certain the runs were enough, holding the Pioneers to seven hits, while striking out ten. Behind the backstop, the hundred or so Chester fans rose to their feet, arms raised as the last out was made.

Girlfriends shrieked, young boys looked on enviously, proud dads high-fived, hugging each other, faces beaming as if their sons were heroes.

The players shook hands with the losing team, took a brief team picture, and began to celebrate. Dog piling their longtime coach and teacher, the boys could finally say it—even scream it: "Regional Champions!"

Back Row L-R: Coach Stan Newby, Brad Butler, Jarrod Peters, Bobber, Zach Engel, Jake Arbeiter, Coach Jeremy Williamson, Coach Kordys
Middle Row L-R: Mike Knop, Bundy Brown, Bruce Luthy, Josh Hecht, Doc
Front Row L-R: Derek Link, Herb, Eric Caby, Phil Grau, Jeremy Blechle, Phil Shields

CHAPTER NINETEEN
Basketball Night

Basketball is the one sport where you must perform a skilled task of multiple body movements, including fakes, with a ball and under the pressure of someone trying to prevent you from doing so, in front of 1,000 people, half of them taunting you, and in what amounts to your underwear. Take away the crowd, and remove half the underwear and you have Monday night pickup games at the Chester courts, shirts versus skins.

The Chester outdoor playground, where Bobber and his brother held court

Two days following the regional win, a new season

was beginning in Chester, and it did not include a ball consisting of a small rubber core, wrapped in yarn, covered with leather, and held together by tightly wound red string.

Monday nights at the outdoor Chester basketball courts were a rite of passage for many youngsters growing up in the tough little river town. The first day of each week beginning in May and ending in August from 6:00 p.m. to 11:00 p.m. marked the start of what was known around the county as "Basketball Night."

High school, college, and adult aged men from all over Randolph County and across the Mississippi in towns such as Perryville, Ste. Genevieve, and Cape Girardeau, would make their way to the giant leaning cage that enclosed a green all-purpose basketball court for Monday night 5 on 5, "win and you play" basketball at the Chester courts. The premise was simple: bring a team and win. Be the first to fifteen, and your team gets to run all night.

The concrete court and the flexible stainless steel mesh, almost as tall as the white metal backboards, and the broken padlocks gave an aura of—the comparison could not be avoided—ghetto. Or prison. It spoke of toughness, mean streets. But this was small town toughness, and any fight that broke out was among, usually, relatives.

The warm nights of summer and the absence of officiating brought out the best and the worst for pure battle and play, the likes of which, as every dad complained, was being lost in American baseball when every game had to be organized by adults who fitted their children in professional looking uniforms before they had even played the game. With only one court for play, competition was fierce. If you failed to bring a suitable team or weren't lucky enough to earn a spot, you'd sit for three hours just watching. The courts were the provenance of local folklore. A thunderous dunk or game-winning three could turn an ordinary man into an instant legend.

The brothers, Bobber and Jason, they couldn't wait for their Monday night ritual to begin. The two had been part of "The Game" almost since its inception five years earlier, before it had attracted the best players from both sides of the river.

Back from a one year stint in the junior college ball scene, Jason was close to the top of his game when it came to the sport. Bobber, however, hadn't touched a *basket*ball in three months.

"Slow down and eat your food," Sharon insisted as the two brothers scarfed down their potatoes and meatloaf. It was Monday, May 25, and the first night of pick-up ball.

"Can't," said Jason with a mouthful. "We have to get to the courts by six if we want to get the first game."

"You're not going to play, are you?" Sharon turned to her middle son and asked. "You've got baseball on Thursday."

"I'll just hang out and see who shows," Bobber replied. "I bet Jarrod and some of the other guys are there."

As the boys put on their sneaks and hurried out the door, Bobber realized he had forgotten something. "Hold up, I got to go back in and get my brace," he said.

"I didn't think you were going to play!" Jason said.

Bobber pretended not to hear. It didn't take long to retrieve a roll of athletic tape and the knee brace that had held his knee together through the high school basketball season. "Alright, let's go."

Jason shifted the stick of his sub-woofer packed Isuzu into first. Lyrics flowed from the Trooper's amped up speakers.

"Got me worried, stressin, my vision's blurred/
The question is will I live? No one in the world loves me/
I'm headed for danger, don't trust strangers…/
Don't wanna make excuses, cause this is how it is/
What's the use unless we're shootin' no one notices the youth/
It's just me against the world, baby."

Jason and Bobber's teammates were choice. They were the goons. There was Hittmeier, a junior college player in Olney, Illinois, who grew up in Chester and had been a court regular for years. His tenacious driving to the basket and his competitive nature made him a force on many hot summer nights. Tejada, a 6'5" lanky twig was a pure set shooter who used other players' bullish drives to his advantage. Setting up mostly on the three-point line, Tejada would wait patiently for a kick out pass and rarely miss the open triple.

The combination of the brothers, Hittmeier's tenacity, Tejada's shooting, and a fifth man, Micah Reiman, who could rebound anything they missed, and they held the court on Monday nights against the finest talent in a four-county area.

The Trooper pulled into the high school parking lot, and Jason jammed it in park. The trio made the short walk across the tennis courts and through the chain length gate leading into the court. A crowd had already begun to gather.

It looked as if all the regulars had made it out. Hansbury, a thirty year old former high school Yellow Jacket, famous for his left-handed ball fakes and up and under moves, Marino, a local drunk ready for his weekly exercise and spot up three-point attempts, Larry Byrd, a local Gilster's lead man by day, and gangly court swing man by night, Berner, a short, three-point specialist, capable of shooting from anywhere on the court, and Caldwell, a tenacious 6'2", 220 pound Charles Barkley type, would be the first competition of the night for the team of five.

The makeshift squad of Chester regulars provided little competition for the team constructed mainly for the long run of the night to come. Marino's desperation heaves fell short, Byrd's drives led to steals or blocked shots at the hands of Hittmeier, Hansbury's up and under moves fooled no one, swatted away by the long-armed Tejada, Caldwell only managed a couple buckets, and Berner a couple threes in the losing effort.Up next were the "Rock Throwers" from across the river, 6"5" and 6'10" brothers from Perryville, fresh off college seasons, along with another college guy from Cape Girardeau, and a high school duo from St. Genevieve.

Trading one three after another, the brothers, after hitting seven in a row, had built a 14–4 lead on what was, after all, their home court. An exclamation steal and breakaway dunk by Hittmeier sent the onlookers into a fury. The boys from Missouri were put down before they could get loose.

While celebrating the dunk that polished off the "Rock Throwers," beats from the souped up sound systems rang from an approaching caravan of cars. "Hey, boys, look who's got next," said Micah. A gang from Sparta had pulled up.

The Spartans looked like they had been lifting weights for a living. Beefed up, the crew from the town on the north end of the county were no boys. These were grown ass men, and they wanted next. Two of them played in college. And they brought with them one other aspect that commanded respect on the basketball court: they were black.

"What up, Keeve?" Hittmeier greeted the familiar leader of the Sparta squad. "You all got next."

This game was not going to be like any other game played on the court that night. This was going to be the best Sparta had to offer versus the best Chester had to offer, and everyone in attendance knew it.

The Spartans didn't take a single shot to warmup. Rather, they dunked. If this was meant as a greeting of intimidation, it partially worked. "Shi*ii*t," Jason whispered to his little brother. The rims of the Chester court had seen few dunks over the years from those Germanic Caucasians whose ancestors had settled in the Mississippi valley. They were only slightly off level from the day they were first bolted to the glass.

"Who's shooting do or die?" asked Keeve.

"Go ahead, my man," Hittmeier said, gesturing chivalrously. Keeve hit the three, chose skins for his team and took the north basket which after warmups seemed to gape like the mouth of a bass. Jason and Bobber and their tall teammates said, "Okay," and put on their muscle shirts for battle—the battle that became known as the "greatest pick-up game ever" on the courts of Chester.

The Sparta captain immediately went to his hesitation crossover dribble, leaving the taller Hittmeier flat-footed. Driving the lane, Keeve saw clear glass. But Bobber saw it coming and had shuffled over for help defense, planted his feet with the quick one-two stop and mousey squeak from his Adidas. Keeve avoided the charge, letting go of the ball with a practiced lob to the rim. Out of nowhere, Sparta's big man slammed it home, shaking the entire backboard.

"You guys won't be runnin' much longer," the Spartans informed them. "Chester ain't shit."

Always audacious in the face of a challenge, Bobber had learned the hard way over the years—on blacktops and backyards and sweaty summer gyms. He wanted the ball. Inbounding quickly, Jason fed to his little brother on the wing. Bobber set up for the shot. It took only a second. "Two one," he announced. Three-point shots were worth two points—100% more than non-threes—and as Jason and Bobber, who had learned their math on Monopoly boards, knew: always shoot the three. It was worth not 3/2's more 2/1 more.

The battle turned personal. The teams were trading insults along with buckets, and no one was calling fouls. The pride of your town pride was at stake. The pride of family was on the line.

Besides, the girls were watching. They twined their fingers in the flexible steel mesh or sat cross-legged on the hot concrete.

The Chester courts on Monday nights were as much a social as an athletic setting, like the boxing venues of Las Vegas. Only here, in the humid river valley, the girls came not in PETA fur and diamonds, but nipple-tented summer blouses and short jean shorts whose soft fringe tickled the peek of her ass pressed on the hot concrete.

The shining tattooed torsos of the Spartans glistened with sweat. Chester's muscle shirts were sopped. It was win by two, the fifteen point game in overtime. With the score 20–19, Chester up one, Jason whispered to his little brother as they backpeddled to the north end.

"Let 'm shoot."

The plan: give Sparta the perimeter shot. They were tiring, and Jason knew a hospitable invitation would look inviting. No one in four counties would dare *not* take a shot if challenged by an opponent. Not with girls watching. Keeve took the invite—missed and Reiman grabbed the board.

Reiman's outlet pass found the younger brother. Bobber dribbled with a burst of speed, was surprised by the open lane to the basket and went to the rim—heard two beasts close on him before he saw their glistening bodies. Jumping as high as his skinny legs could take him, Bobber faked the layup and kicked it out to his brother. He knew where Jason would be. It was his spot. The spot he owned in their own backyard like Park Place. Bobber's arms were signaling victory before the ball swished through the wet net.

But for Bobber the celebration was only a moment.

"What's wrong, man?" Jason asked his little brother, who was limping toward the gate. "You hurt or somethin'?"

"I'll be fine," Bobber lied.

"Take my keys and go on home. You have Sectionals."

The Spartans sat back against the mesh, guzzling Gatorade, their pecs and rippled torsos still glistening. Bobber turned and mouthed to them what his mom always said: "Can't you do something about it?"

CHAPTER TWENTY
"These Jackets fine for any season."

"Hey," Bobber told The Brothers the next day at practice. "I heard a story once that John Wayne Gacy used to poke his head through the bars and give baseball advice to our dads."

"Who's John Wayne Gacy?"

"He's the guy who strangled all those boys."

"He ain't no Major Leaguer."

"The guy who dressed up as a clown?"

Gacy, the worst criminal in Illinois history had been executed five years earlier, of course, after a quality stay at Chester's finest facility, the Menard State Penitentiary. In his Chicago suburb, he had lured unsuspecting boys into his home, strangled them, and buried them in the basement.

"What'd he tell them?"

"He said to choke up on the bat."

The truth was the prison where Danny Ohlau and many of the dads worked was just about the opposite of the ball field where the boys had gathered for their last few practices before Sectionals. They were two different worlds though both circumscribed by fence. The kind of vigilance the dads held standing along the third base fence watching their sons had only one thing in common with that of the prison: patience. Eternal patience.

The team had only four days to savor their school's first ever regional championship. Chester boasted a record of 27–2, best in the entire southern part of the state. It seemed, after winning on a big stage, the Jackets were starting to get the respect from the sportswriters whose lack of attention had only motivated them more for most of the season.

In fact, as if to make up for his own oversight, Jim Gordillo decided it was time to feature this year's Jackets in a front-page column, the first ever for a baseball team from the small river town. The fifth-hour scholars of Chester High did not have to go flapping through the paper in search of their names. The headline read with the same quaint style that eight-lady bridge clubs, where always "a good time was had by all," were reported on in many an Illinois small town paper: "These Jackets fine for any season," Gordillo gloated.

The article featured Peters, Luthy, Knop, and Bobber as multiple sport standouts. Like most small towns of similar size, double or triple dipping was necessary when it came to sports. It held true for all sports at CHS. If the track, basketball, and baseball players didn't play football, or vice versa, there wouldn't have been competitive squads in any of the sports. So Jarrod Peters was Chester's pitcher/shortstop, quarterback, and forward on the basketball team, while Luthy was third baseman and offensive lineman, Knop, second baseman, small forward and defensive back, and Bobber, pitcher/first base, shooting guard, and distance runner on the cross country team.

Although they were getting recognized, their opponents were yet still admired more. Rightfully so, Chester had yet to accomplish anything outside their own region.

"Class A baseball sectionals kick off today," the *Southern* announced anew the morning of Saturday, May 29. "Sectional newcomer Chester (27–2) takes on tradition-laden Alton Marquette (20–10) in the 10 a.m. opener, while Nashville (31–5) and Columbia (20–9) duke it out in the second semi." The boys read on with an intensity and focus they hadn't since the ACT. "Alton Marquette had been a baseball power in the 1980s. The 1999 Explorers are not bad either," the article deliberately understated.

It was a long quiet bus ride that early Saturday morning. The bus, more reserved than usual, carried a dozen or so high school minds now empty of all schoolwork, young men, four of them now old enough to be drafted, in the mood of a mission. The bus hummed along like an old WWII bomber.

Upon reaching their destination, the boys lurched from their meditations. Taking the field was the only cure for their nerves. As soon as their feet hit the infield dirt for warmups, they all felt better. They were, after all, the Top Seed.

Bobber was slated as the starting pitcher for what was going to be the most important game he had ever been asked to pitch. Trotting to the mound for warm-ups in the top of the first, he could feel the pain in his knee from that fake layup against the Spartans. Jason had come home and helped him ice it, and for a couple days, he walked gingerly, mostly trying to ignore the issue. But whatever pain he might have had quickly subsided as he began warming up. He could hear the Marquette hitters as they were taking their swings and murmuring near the visiting dugout. He sensed the conversation stop and felt their eyes upon him.

Whether it was the fact that he was already loose, the uncertainty of his leg, or the mind games he was attempting to play with the enemy batters, Bobber continued lobbing pitches toward the plate as the Explorers looked on. He thought he heard one of them scoff. Bobber responded by lobbing one in there, a fat piece of fruit. Temptation bound in white leather and stitched with red thread. But a core of — deception.

After the seventh of his eight warm-up pitches, almost all of the Alton players were watching. "That can't be his fastball, can it?" one of them said, deliberately too loud.

"We are gonna rock him," they agreed and sent their leadoff man up.

As the first Explorer hitter made his way into the box, eager to take his cuts against the skinny lefty with the soft warmups, Bobber knew he had to set a precedent from the start and show the boys from the "North" his view of what pitching really was.

He could feel that he had his good stuff from the very first pitch. And his leg felt fine. His curve fell in for strike one. The next pitch, gripping it a little softer, a changeup, sailed high—but looked so fat that the Alton leadoff man took a hard, undisciplined cut right through it.

Bobber would now mix it up more. Placing more weight onto his drive leg allowed him to generate an increase in the energy of the ball exiting his hand. These at least were the semitechnical explanations his dad had drilled into him. But today there was no time for science: it was the art of pitching.

The four-seam pitch zipped right past the unsuspecting hitter. Although only reaching a mediocre 78 mph on the gun, the pitch seemed more like 88 to baffled hitters. Grumbling and striking his bat on the ground, the leadoff man trudged back to the dugout without any advice to Number 2. He had no idea what he had just witnessed.

The next batter fared no better, nor the next, nor the next. The young, soft throwing lefty, carried a no-hitter through four as Chester brought a 4–0 lead into the fifth after Derek Link, the Jacket nine hitter, belted a two-run home run in the fourth, Chester's school record fiftieth home run of the season.

Marquette made it interesting in the sixth, getting the first two hitters on and managing to bring them home. But with the tying run on deck and a runner at third, Bobber preserved the victory.

News travels fast in a town like Chester. By the time Omer got the players home around one in the afternoon, it seemed everyone in town knew. Parents, fans, and students alike were waiting for the team behind CHS. A hundred people was a huge crowd in a small town. The boys felt like pro athletes or rock stars stepping off that bus.

"I know we won, but we haven't won anything yet," Jarrod turned to Bobber and said. "Yeah, no kidding, I hope they're as excited after Monday's game." "I wonder who we'll play?"

The matter of the Sectional finals was on Kordys' mind the entire next afternoon. When he finally heard who the Yellow Jackets would face, he didn't know whether to feel uneasy or excited. The name "Nashville" elicited no thoughts of Country Western music now, but the slight ping in the stomach of facing a familiar foe.

Nashville had shown no weaknesses in dispatching Columbia High School in the one o'clock game. The Hornets, once again led by a strong pitching performance from Brock Holston and a two home run, four RBI performance from Borowiak, set up what was going to be a rubber game for the two S.I.R.R. teams. It would determine once and for all who would represent the entire southern part of the state at the State Tournament.

How do you prepare for the biggest day of your life? That was the question The Brothers were pondering, lying in their beds late Sunday night. *Should I have gone out tonight? Should we go to the cages before the game tomorrow? Should we eat the same foods we ate before the Marquette game? What side of the bed should I get up on?* For the seniors, the questions were even more fateful: *Is this going to be the last game I ever play in*? Many thoughts troubled the sleep of the Jacket players before the biggest game of their baseball careers.

As Monday morning rolled around, Danny Ohlau, always the critic when it came to his sons' athletic endeavors, saw something during the Marquette game that needed attention.

Knowing his son, the fact that he was "pull happy"—prone to pulling his shoulder when swinging—Danny had a plan for the morning of the final.

The bus wasn't set to leave school until 11:00 a.m. for the 1:00 p.m. start time in Marissa. He was going to take his son to the cages. "Taking swings off the old one wheel has got to help," Danny told his son. "Borowiak sure throws a straight fastball."

Sharon had fed Bobber his favorite breakfast, and now his dad fed him ball after ball into the pitching machine. Bobber's swing had never looked so smooth nor felt so good. Five buckets later, blisters were starting to form on his hands. "We might not want to swing you out today," his dad said. "Let's get you to the bus."

Danny drove his recently acquired late grandpa's forest green, 1974 El Camino straight to the school. Seeming to understand the relevance of the moment, Danny turned to his son. "Enjoy yourself today. This type of thing doesn't come around very often." And just before Bobber boarded the bus, he heard the El Camino honk.

CHAPTER TWENTY-ONE
The Wind Blowing In

If you win, you'll never remember. If you lose, you'll remember for the rest of your life. In a split second, your life is divided in two.

The Jackets were four wins away from the ultimate prize. Beyond the swagger and the confidence, what was most annoying to the opposing teams was the fact that these boys from Chester were good, very good. "This team could be the best in the state, 1A or 2A it doesn't matter," fans and commentators were heard saying throughout the packed grounds at Marissa's Schulte Field.

By this time, the Jackets were ranked first in the entire Southern Illinois region at 27–2 and quickly emerging as State Championship favorites. Bobber, hitting over .500 with 4 homers and 44 RBIs and had a 9–1 record on the mound with a 2.65 ERA, Peters sported a .460 batting average with 13 homers and 41 RBIs, and carried an 8–0 record on the mound with a 2.63 ERA, while third baseman Bruce Luthy was hitting a cool .512 with 6 homers and 36 RBIs. In the heart of the order, the Chester Yellow Jackets turned half their at bats into hits. Then came the timely hitting of Bundy, Herb, Knop, and Z.

Grampa Knop had the bus humming up Route 4 to Marissa. The black fields along the way were rowed with new sprung blades of corn. From the front seat of the bus, on his way to the most important game of his coaching career, Kordys turned around to observe just how close his team had become over the year. Sitting in the second seat from the back, Peters turned to look too at the teammates he knew he might never play with again.

One of only four seniors on the team, Jarrod was feeling the weight of the day's game more than most. Sitting there on the quiet, peaceful bus, hearing the engine purring and feeling the warm, late spring air carrying through the half-open windows, making their way through the Randolph County countryside, watching through the window the blur of young green corn and soybean fields, he thought about endings. The game today could be his last as a high schooler—then he quickly barred that thought. High school itself had already ended. Graduation had already come and gone, and all the emotions with it. But baseball was still on. Baseball still lived. Peters screwed his road-beaten cap on tighter. He had traded Herb.

~~~

Jarrod Peters doing what he did best

Monday, May 31, 1999

Schulte field was simply ordinary. It had a manicured grass infield, short 310 foot porches in left and right, gaps measuring 340 feet, just left of the sign over the scoreboard letting everybody know exactly where they were, and a center field fence that read 380. It sported six rows of covered bleachers that extended around the backstop giving fans an ideal spot to either get some shade or escape the rain that had been forecasted to arrive later in the day.

Over 500 parents, students, and fans filled the stands. Moms unfolded their lawn chairs, and the dads took their positions along the fence. Barbeque smells wafted here and there in the uneven wind. Orange and blue shirts colored the bleachers and baselines to cheer on the River to River rivals.

Nerves began tightening when one of The Brothers glanced behind the backstop. Bo Collins, coach at Southern Illinois University in Edwardsville, and Neil Fiala, former St. Louis Cardinal and local junior college coach, were sitting together there. Next to them sat a larger gentleman wearing a Kansas City Royals cap and another gentleman holding a clipboard and a radar gun. He too had a Cardinals hat on.

"Wonder who they are here to see?" the boys asked one another. No matter who it was, the fact that they were there at all was a reminder of just how far the team had come.

On this afternoon there would be no surprise about who would take the mound against the Jackets. It was going to be Borowiak. Although ace Brock Holston had thrown the first round game, Borowiak wasn't a drop off. He lacked Holston's off-speed arsenal but was excellent with his control—in spite of his last outing against Chester. He holstered a steady fastball, which could reach the mid to upper eighties and had the radar guns in the stands raised. Just as important at this level of play, Borowiak possessed a bull dog's mentality on the mound.

"We knew coming in that Zach [Borowiak] was going to have his best stuff." Kordys would later tell the reporters. "It was going to be up to us to hit it."

As expected, the game started off as a pitching duel. After allowing the first two Nashville hitters to reach base, Peters went from mean to meaner. He retired the next three, including the great Borowiak himself.

Now on the mound, Borowiak reciprocated. He coaxed Bundy into flying out, struck out Grau looking, and deadened Peters bat in a ground out to short. Then, after another flawless top half by Peters, now throwing his meanest, "Little Bruce" stepped in to lead off the bottom of the second.

Big Bruce gripped the fence along the third base line.

As Little Luthy worked his cleats into the box, he heard a familiar voice ringing out from the dugout. "Let's go, Poop!" Peters was standing in the doorway to the cellar. This was becoming a very personal game.

Luthy had uncharacteristically struggled through most of the Sectional, trying to find the swing that had earned him All-Southern Illinois honors for the regular season.

"Let's go, Poop! Get it started!" joined in Skorcz from his manager's position on the bench, his stutter gone.

The first two pitches from Borowiak were pure gas. Falling into a quick 0–2 hole, swinging late on the two heaters, Luthy was lost. Big Bruce began to pace nervously on the sideline.

Following up the two fastballs with a flawless circle changeup on the outside corner sent the Jacket senior walking back to the dugout, disgusted with himself.

"It's okay, man," Bobber called from the on-deck circle, betraying no fear. "I'll pick you up."

Knocking the doughnut off his beloved Redline,

Bobber sauntered to the plate. He wasn't going to let Borowiak even know he knew his name. During two seasons of battling each other in varsity basketball, Bobber had come to respect but at the same time detest Borowiak for being so talented and fortunate. To Bobber, the Nashville boys were nothing like he and his friends. Chester boys considered themselves self-made players from a tough, prison town. Nashville, a nice little farm community and county seat, seemed cushy.

Coyly making his way into the chalked rectangle, Bobber had one picture replaying in his head: the countless balls shot towards his bat only a couple hours prior in the Cohen cage. He was training his thoughts to expect such a pitch from Borowiak. *He sure throws a straight fastball ...*

Bobber dug in, as close to the plate as he could without being considered out of the box. His plan, to entice the Hornet into throwing a fastball, worked. As the pitch approached, time seemed to slow.

His hard, effortless swing made perfect contact with the ball. Exploding off the bat at a 45-degree angle toward center field, the ball suddenly began carrying with the swift westerly wind toward the gap in left. It seemed to hang forever. Then it flew over the 380 sign. In the bleachers, the Chester fans sprung up, the orange and black flags waving in the warm spring breeze, cowbells ringing out down the line. Yes, cowbells. If anyone wanted to smirk about the country bumpkins from Chester, let 'em. The whole town was proud as hell.

Bobber crosses the plate after hitting a home run off Borowiak

As the game continued, Chester threatened again in the third. Taking advantage of a couple Borowiak walks and a wild pitch, runners were now on the corners. But just as Borowiak seemed to be struggling he drew strength from somewhere and struck out Peters to end the rally. The cowbells clanked to silence.

Two innings later, in the fifth, Bobber came to bat again. Again, he challenged Borowiak to throw his best pitch and again the smoothest swing he'd ever felt carried the ball high and far. The Nashville right fielder turned and ran toward the fence. Everyone in the park stared at one disappearing gray-white dot. Suddenly, a brisk wind knocked it down. It was caught on the warning track.

But if moral victories count, both sides claimed one on the play. "Nice hit!" Bobber heard his mom uncharacteristically shout from the stands. He was willing to overlook the technical inaccuracy.

In the top of the sixth, Peters continued his dealing on the mound. With Bobber's second-inning home run still the only hit on the books, it seemed as if each team had succumbed to a batter's disease.

With his team struggling to get going, Coach David Vieth, a former high school baseball star himself at Illinois baseball power Edwardsville, decided to revert to a strategy from the good ol' days of baseball.

When the Nashville nine-hitter and catcher, Ryan Dinkelman, led off the inning with a walk, their leadoff hitter, Cruser, came to the plate. With the Hornets down a run, and hitless on the day, there was only one thing to do. Vieth gave a sign. Kordys gave a sign. The Chester boys were being warned to look for the bunt. Indeed, Cruser squared quickly at the plate, and Bobber and Poop charged from their corners.

Cruser sent the bunt trickling down the first base line. Bobber got to it easily—but instead of taking the easy out, flipping the ball to Peters who knew to cover first, he opted for getting the lead runner at second. Dinkelman, only halfway there, stood no chance of making it safely.

It was a throw that Bobber had made ten thousand times in his life. He had thrown it to his dad on the farm. Principal Lochead had seem him throw it on the playground. The Sheriff and Kordys trusted in his arm more than anyone else's on the team. But the throw in the direction of shortstop Jeremy Blechle at second sailed errantly over Blechle's head and into left center field. Scooting to third was Dinkelman, while Cruser cruised into second.

Again, Vieth signaled. Nashville's number two hitter, Travis Klingler laid down a bunt of his own. Traveling to the front of the mound, the ball found Peters. Fielding it, Peters lost his footing and fell to his back and short-armed a throw to Z at the plate. But the scampering Dinkelman scored, and Cruser ended up on third, Klingler on second.

Then came Borowiak. The Yellow Jackets had suppressed the first team All-Stater for almost two games. He was due. He slapped a two-RBI double to right center. A ground ball and yet another bunt—a gutsy suicide play—and the Hornets were suddenly up 4–1. The momentum had shifted. Vieth's bunting had paid off. It seemed almost unfair, desperate, like fighting with the butt of the rifle because you had no more ammunition, but for Nashville it worked. The passive bat had become the most ironic of weapons.

When the Jackets got their chance, they seemed anxious at the plate. This time there was to be no mid-game rally. One Jacket hitter after another went down, duffing weak ground balls or looking at strike three.

In the bottom of the seventh came a glimmer of hope: Knop, with one out, was able to scratch out a single. The cowbells clanged. The Chester fans were on their feet. A cool breeze billowed windbreakers and uniforms, a spring storm approaching quickly from the west. Everyone tried to read it, the weather. Hope looks to signs. Knop took his lead off first. The cowbells clanged louder.

But Borowiak, the scouts' guns trained on his fastball, had one final pitch in him. A sinking fastball and quick double play ended the game, and just like that a dream ended. Lightning struck in the distance.

A feeling of great, irrecoverable loss, even tragedy, overwhelmed the sons of Chester, and the storm that enclosed the entire southern Illinois sky at the bottom of the last inning could not have been crueler. There was no consolation in the dugout nor hiding. There The Brothers and the seniors inexpressibly grieved, looking vaguely to each other for how to. The storm now closed in, the sky quickly turning dark and the heavens spoke angrily. Lightning and thunder conspired against them. Heavy drops of rain mixed with the tears on their faces. Kordys told them how proud he was of them in a speech he had not practiced.

The fans made for their cars.

As the young men exited the dugout, their heads still down but not caring about the rain, there was waiting for them the one thing that had not failed them all season: their fathers.

Dan Ohlau was there and The Warden (Knop's dad). The Sheriff (Peters' dad) hugged his son, and Big Bruce his namesake. Floyd Engel (Z's dad) and Mike Seymour (Herb's dad), Norm Grau (Phil's dad) and Fred Davitz (Doc's dad) were there. Their fathers told them, "You have nothing to be ashamed of." And, words that meant nothing at the time, everything later, "We are proud of you." That is, we are proud to be your fathers.

With one lift of the arm Dan placed his hand on Bobber's shoulder whispering in his ear. "If anybody had to lose the game," his father told him, with a sense of destiny and finality that it takes nearly a lifetime to learn, "I would have wanted it to be you."

Bobber swung around. "Why?"

"Because I know you can handle it."

The bus ride home from Marissa was not part of time but only of memory. It was a ride they would remember for the rest of their years, the ride home that every team in the state but one must take.

As Grampa Knop ground the gears and the big yellow bus pulled away, some came to partial realization of the loss. Things were moving on. Others, however, found that acceptance impossible. The dream was still there, long formed inside them. For Bobber, who could never cry, stoic like his father, there was no name for the feeling. Only years later when he heard Father Dennis read from the Scriptures "A sword will pierce your own heart too," the words that the angel spoke to the Virgin Mary, and he saw a picture of the Lord on the cross, His side pierced, His Mother on her knees reaching helplessly up to the Son, did Bobber find an image for his pain. Could there ever be victory in loss? Life in death? In time he would come to know why Sharon Ohlau insisted her children grow up three doors down from St. Mary's.

Every year, every team but one must take that long ride home. There he was, alone in his seat and lost in himself. The boy who had waited his whole life for one moment at the end of one glorious day, who had gutted out ten wins on the mound, none more important than the one two days earlier, who had hit over .500 at the plate, leading the team in more categories than the runs batted in, making countless plays in the field, blamed himself. "How can I have let that throw get away like that?" he began to punish himself with the blame. "Why couldn't I just have made the play?"

No caravan of fans escorted the team home, no police paraded them through town, no celebration awaited them when they returned home to Chester. When Grampa Knop pulled the quiet bus to a stop at the back of the school, most of the boys had no trouble exiting. Bobber, however, remained in his seat. He had never felt so alone in his life.

But he wasn't alone.

Peters was there, sitting behind him. Peters too had given his all. The two sat in silence for what seemed like an hour before Kordys called to the back. There was something finally comforting in Kordys' businesslike tone.

"Time to go home, boys."

Stepping off the bus, Bobber was hit by a gust of rainy wind. The same wind, the thought suddenly occurred to him, that had held his homer in.

BOX SCORE:

Nashville 4, Chester 1

Nashville   000040 0–4 3 0

Chester   010000 0–1 2 2

Borowiak and Dinkelman. Peters and Engel. W-Borowiak (7–0). L-Peters (8–1). Hitters – Nashville: Cruser 1–4, Klingler 1–4 (BI), Borowiak 1–4 (2BI), Holston 0–1 (BI); Chester: Ohlau 1–3 (HR, BI), Knop 1–3.

PART FOUR: EPILOGUE

Looking Back, Going Forward

"It was never just a game for us. It will be with us forever, for better or for worse.

The rising warmth of the spring, the leather pop of the mitt, the crack and ping of the bat, the sound of children playing in the sandlot, will bring back to memory the game that for an entire childhood seemed what life was meant to be."

—Craig "Bobber" Ohlau

If you were to drive down Route 3 from St. Louis into Chester, Cohen Field would be visible just before you enter town on the left-hand side of the road. The grounds have changed a little in the last fifteen years. Not much change has occurred to the two baseball fields that hosted so much drama in the 1999 season, but the park now boasts a few additions. Softball fields, soccer fields, and a walking track equipped with different checkpoints for exercise complement the two baseball fields in the center.

If you drive into town, turning left at the four-way stop at Hardees and travel down Swanwick, you would reach the high school. Little about the school has changed over the years with the exceptions of the revamped weight room and renovations to the revered football field. However, there is much reason for pride.

As you walk into the double doors en route to the school's Colbert gymnasium, visitors are greeted by wall to wall plaques honoring Chester High's long-time greats: the exceptional football, track, and basketball teams of the past are honored, and, as you examine the walls and trophy cases one picture stands out among the others. You see your buddies, The Brothers, you see your coach, you see the past.

Peters, arguably the best power hitter ever to step foot in the small high school, got his chance in college. After a successful two years at Division I junior college power Southwestern Illinois College, where he was an All-Conference pitcher, he earned a spot as a scholarship pitcher at Southern Illinois University in Edwardsville. At SIUE he worked his way into the starting rotation, improving each year. Peaking at 93 mph on the radar gun his senior year, his fastball attracted the attention of the pro scouts, but come draft day, nobody called. Ready to move on after graduating, Peters moved home, and is now raising a family while working for the county as a cop, much like his father before him, The Sheriff. He loves his job.

Phil Grau played college ball way down in Tyler, Texas, afterward drifting around the Independent League baseball scene, ultimately quitting after a few years.

Bruce Luthy also played ball after high school. He attended Lindenwood University in St. Charles, Missouri, playing two years there before exiting the game he loved. He too moved back home and now works at a local bank.

Doc, Herb, and James, nearly inseparable growing up, are still very close today, all three still residing in close proximity, raising kids of their own in the town on the bluff. The trio can frequently be seen gathered together in their favorite local bar or visiting each other's homes, reminiscing of their earlier times together.

Time sped up for Bobber after that junior year. He was one of the top runners in the conference in cross country his senior year, in basketball led the conference in scoring at 24 points per game, a school record, and, although The Brothers and the Chester Jackets lost in the Regionals, Bobber was at the top of the southern Illinois leaders in hitting with a .547 average.

Bobber followed Jarrod, his friend and longtime teammate to a junior college, enticed by the dream of winning an NJCAA national championship. There, Bobber led the team in runs scored, walks, and stolen bases while hitting .340. Their team came within one run of advancing to the Junior College World Series.

After ACL surgery and a redshirt year, Bobber headed to Southern Illinois University in Edwardsville. At SIUE, against some of the best college pitching in the Midwest, Bobber batted third for the Cougars and lead the team in almost every hitting category over his three years there. Pro scouts began to take notice.

The scouting notes looked surprisingly like the scorecard Bobber, Doc, and Herb had made so many years earlier, trying out their grade school classmates:

Scout Notes:
Hitting ability–90, Power–50, Running Speed–60, Base

Running–50, Arm Strength–30, Arm Accuracy–80, Fielding–70, Range–50.

Player's Strengths: size, athleticism, hitting for average, good bat speed, selective at the plate, consistency, doesn't strike out.

Player's Weaknesses: minus arm, too selective at plate, bum right leg, content.

Although he was listed on the draft cards of local scouts, no team was willing to take a chance on the broken down lefty hitter. Then one day, after a two-week professional tryout, Bobber decided he'd had enough of his dream of making it in the pro game and just like that, he quit.

Using his degree, he took a high school teaching and coaching job. Years later he still holds onto the game he loves, hobbling around the bases in a semi-pro league and showing off for the high school team he coaches. When his students ask him what happened in his baseball career or why he didn't make it to the "Bigs," he always answers without regrets. "It's simple boys. I obviously wasn't good enough," he smiles, "And aren't you guys lucky I wasn't, 'cause if I was, you all wouldn't have me around as your coach."

Yet one dream can give way to another. She had just returned from a summer back home in Millstadt, Illinois, where she was a lifeguard at the local swimming pool. One could see what the sun had done to her legs and hair, her long blonde hair that hugged her back. Her toned, tan legs glistened in the lights of the gym as she walked past. After a couple minutes of agonizing deliberation, Bobber decided he had to at least walk over and say something to her. As he walked through the gym, about ten feet from the fifteen college girls in gripping spandex, he froze. He wasn't always the best at talking to the girls. But here he was compelled. Freshman year, he had dated the best looking girl in school and went a month without even kissing her, because he liked her so much. She broke up with him because she said he was boring. If only he could be as thrilling as the thrill he felt...

He could only muster up enough courage to smile as he made his way past the blonde hair, blue-eyed, tanned legged girl. Her name was Heather. She looked back at him with a commensurate smile. He was hoping the smile meant something.

A year later, they married.

Together they have two daughters, Madelyn and Jocelyn, and a son, Peyton.

Peyton doesn't know about the dream. Not yet.

Today, Bobber's feelings about his high school days remain complicated, unfulfilled, like a feeling that is lost inside him, stored deep in memory. Like most of his friends and old teammates, he can't stop thinking about what they didn't accomplish in the final year of the century, the last chance.

"Daddy, Daddy, can you show me the book?" Peyton asks excitedly, wrapping his tiny arms around his father's legs. He is three.

He doesn't know about the dream. Not yet.

Bobber picks up his son, looking him in the eye, pausing for a brief moment, smiling. "Sure, Buddy. Let me show you a little something about your dad."

With Peyton on his lap, the father turns a page into the past.

"That's Daddy," Bobber points out, touching the boy in the photo who does not yet know what it is like to have his heart broken. Losing interest after only a couple pages, Peyton fidgets to return to his dinosaur models and Hot Wheels on the floor. His dad lowers him to the floor.

"Here, Daddy." Peyton has his ball. He tosses it, his arms flailing. Is there not something reminiscent there, a hint of either the past or the future or both, the way his little arm, which so often embraces your leg at the knee, flies forward in a natural follow-through?

Peyton runs to get his ball and picks it up as if he had been practicing it for years.

"Thatta boy, Peepers."

He tosses it to his dad.

"Was that a good frow, Dad?"

"Yes," laughs his father, who caught it right at his heart.

The End

Notes

This is a work of nonfiction. It is based primarily on the accounts of those chronicled herein, particularly myself, members of my family, and my friends. Where archival information was available, I relied on it for information, quotes, and the foundation for parts of the narrative. In particular, the coverage by the reporters of the *Chester Herald Tribune* and *Randolph County Journal* as well as by Jim Gordillo and others at the *Southern Illinoisan*.

While I relied upon a number of these sources, most of the research came from revisiting in memory those not so long ago events. Any mistakes are mine and mine alone. Some memories remain fuzzy; others, I suppose, repressed. Some names have been changed to protect— the forgiven.

—Craig Robert Ohlau, the one they call "Bobber."

· · · · ·

But there was one sport above all, one love, as a man loves one thing, one place, even one woman. Baseball.

About the Authors

Craig Ohlau

Craig Ohlau ("Bobber") was born and raised in Chester, Illinois, the setting for the book. In 1995, he and his longtime group of friends won the Khoury League National Championship, and Craig went on to star in baseball at Southern Illinois University in Edwardsville and earn tryouts with several Major League teams. Today, Craig is a writer, coach, teacher and, most importantly, husband and father.

Kevin L. Gingrich

Award-winning writer and scholar (Fulbright nominee) Kevin L. Gingrich, PhD, is the author of numerous publications, ranging from children's stories, feature articles, and columns to scholarly articles, including the pending publication of his dissertation, Parechesis in the Undisputed Pauline. Kevin played Division I sports himself and, like his co-author, suffered the agony of near-miss dreams in Illinois high school state championship play.

Thank you so much for reading one of our **Sports History** novels.
If you enjoyed the experience, please check out our recommended
title for your next great read!

Mickey Mantle: Inside and Outside the Lines by Tom Molito

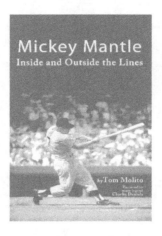

*"Of all the Mantle books that have come out lately, this is the one
that was unique."* —Jeffrey Lasdon, Philanthropist, Lasdon
Pavillion at Lincoln Center:

View other Black Rose Writing titles at

www.blackrosewriting.com/books and use promo code **PRINT** to

receive a **20% discount** when purchasing.

CPSIA information can be obtained
at www.ICGtesting.com
Printed in the USA
LVHW082245110319
610304LV00020B/654/P